Contents

Acknowledgments | viii

01 Saying "I Do" to Becoming a Wedding Planner! | 1
Weddings of Today | 2
Self-Assessment | 2
Recipe for Success | 4
When to Start | 9
Nuts and Bolts | 10
What to Consider Before Taking the Leap | 13

02 Working Out of the Home | 19
Designing Your Space | 19
Wedding Resources | 24
Your Home Environment | 26

03 The Balancing Act | 30
Planning Your Schedule | 30
Sample of Weekly To-Do Lists | 32
Other Commitments | 36

04 Developing Your Business | 41
Setting Up Your Company | 41
Your Business Structure | 42
Research | 45
Creating Your Business Plan | 48

Short-Term Goals | 57

Long-Term Goals | 59

05 Dollars and Sense | 62

Planning for Success | 62

Developing and Using a Budget | 64

Pricing Your Services | 67

Negotiating with Clients and Vendors | 71

Keeping Track of Finances | 72

06 Marketing Your Services | 80

Assessing Who You Are | 80

Developing Your Marketing Materials | 81

Getting Started | 83

Developing a Marketing Plan | 88

07 Running Your Business | 99

What You Need to Know | 101

Enlisting Support | 105

Sourcing Out Your Staffing and Vendor Needs | 106

Staffing Support | 108

Setting-Up Policies | 111

Lining It All Up | 112

08 Legal Matters | 115

Liability | 115

Contracts | 119

Permits and Licenses | 125

Insurance | 126

Improving Your Risk Exposure | 127

Event Ethics | 129

how to start a home-based

Wedding Planning Business

Jill S. Moran, CSEP

Guilford, Connecticut

This book is dedicated to my Mother and Father

Text designed by Sheryl P. Kober

Library of Congress Cataloging-in-Publication Data is available.
Moran, Jill S.
  How to start a home-based wedding planning business / by Jill S. Moran.
    p. cm.
  ISBN 978-0-7627-4939-3
  1. Wedding supplies and services industry. 2. Home-based businesses--Management. 3. Consulting firms--Management. 4. New business enterprises--Management. I. Title. II. Title: Wedding planning business.
  HD9999.W372M67 2009
  392.5068'1--dc22

                        2008039477

Printed in United States of America
10 9 8 7 6 5 4 3 2

09 Wedding Planning Basics | 133

Client Assessment | 133

Face-to-Face Meeting | 134

Putting It in Writing | 135

Critical Elements of Every Wedding | 149

Pulling the Details Together | 151

10 Unique Wedding Trends—The Old and the New | 156

Client Profiles and Personalities | 156

Tried and True | 157

Religious Ceremonies and Cultural Customs | 159

Communication Is Key | 162

Unique Wedding Trends | 163

11 E-Commerce and Internet Use | 176

Starting and Running Your Business | 176

Becoming an Online Resource | 177

Helping Your Clients Get and Stay Connected | 179

Finding Suppliers for Your Weddings | 180

Staying on Top of Wedding Basics and Trends | 181

12 Being the Best | 184

Formal Education | 184

Other Education Options | 188

Above and Beyond | 194

What's Next? | 196

Appendix A: Industry Associations and Educational Resources | 200

Appendix B: Wedding Planning Resources | 214

Index | 220

Acknowledgments

I would like to thank the following people for their assistance with this book:

My interns, Michele Puopolo and Amanda Santucci, for their research and efforts in gathering information to add to this volume. Both students were a breath of fresh air and enthusiasm in my office, and they worked tirelessly to gather the most up-to-date information on wedding planning resources.

My family, for continuing to support my schedule as I juggle the many projects in my life. I thank them for giving me space and time to focus on the ever-changing priorities of each day. I am so fortunate to have their love and acceptance!

My clients, for trusting me with one of the most important celebrations of their lives!

01 Saying "I Do" to Becoming a Wedding Planner!

Just recently, I spent some time at my mother's home, going through some old photos and reminiscing. We came across her wedding album—a beautiful, white leather-bound book filled with photos of my parents' wedding day. There were photos of the church where my brothers and sister and I were baptized, where we received our First Holy Communion and attended masses, weddings, and funerals for loved ones.

My mom and dad had both grown up in our small town, attended school there, and became engaged shortly thereafter. The bridal party was made up of my aunts and uncles, and the guests were friends and family from our small Connecticut town. The reception was held in my grandparents' backyard with a long banquet-style table, covered with a lovely tablecloth and laden with dishes brought by family members to celebrate the happy occasion. That was a snapshot of a wedding of yesteryear.

Fast-forward sixty years. Today's engaged couples most likely meet at college or at work. They often come to the marriage with varied backgrounds—different ethnicities or religions, preferences, friends, hometowns, and expectations of what this magical moment will be. Their guests may travel from across the country (or world) to attend this special event. The couple may pay for the wedding festivities themselves and choose to create a one-of-a-kind getaway for family and friends at an exotic and exclusive location. Today's wedding is an extraordinary experience, quite different from the wedding of my parents' era. It may include fireworks, multiday activities, and thematic elements and entertainment.

Weddings of Today

Enter the wedding planner—aka, orchestral conductor, fairy godmother, Mary Poppins, savior, peacemaker, and emotional therapist. A wedding planner is called on to source out the elements that an engaged couple dreams about, using the resources and talents that he or she has developed, and taking each project to a new level to create an experience unique to each couple. The role of the wedding planner goes beyond contracting with vendors and lining up the wedding party before their march down the aisle. A wedding planner serves as a confidant, a sounding board, and a guide, giving advice and encouragement at times and honesty and a reality check when necessary.

This morphed version of the traditional wedding has left plenty of opportunity for the organized individual who relishes the chance to create new and unique events to celebrate the glorious institution of marriage. So, how do you start? And how do you know if you would be good at the art of wedding planning? Many of us have attended a family wedding, participated as an attendant in a friend's nuptials, or have even ourselves walked down the aisle. If you have become involved in the planning process and have found it exhilarating, perhaps you could make your mark as a professional wedding planner.

Self-Assessment

First, take a realistic look at what intrigues you about wedding planning. Behind the beautiful bride and handsome groom sitting at their sweetheart table at the reception are hours of planning, negotiating, and coordinating. It begins with thoughtful suggestions that build on ideas presented by your client. Sometimes the process leading up to a grand celebration is sprinkled with frustration and angst, both on the part of the client and the planner. To become a successful wedding planner, it takes patience and a sense of humor, as well as organization and a sense of style. One of the most important traits is the ability to know when to listen and when to speak.

Many wedding planners begin their journey in the industry either helping with a friend or family member's wedding or working at a facility or with a vendor who specializes in weddings. Wedding clients differ from corporate or nonprofit clients by adding the personal investment in the experience. They come to the table with a desire to fulfill their personal expectations of the wedding experience. They may also be concerned about the needs of loved ones, and are typically invested from the heart in the entire process. Taking on a wedding client requires a commitment from the planner to ride through the stages from start to finish during times of frustration or fear, anxiety or elation. These emotions will come from the bridal couple and even their family members. You will have multiple "bosses"—brides, grooms, fathers or mothers of the bride and groom, and even others—all with ideas of how the wedding process should go.

If you have played a role in planning a wedding and are excited to do another, and you feel prepared to take on these responsibilities, you may be ready to become a successful wedding planner!

A Picture-Perfect Planner

If you think this is the career for you, look in the mirror and be honest. Enjoying a one-time experience helping someone plan a wedding and actually taking a bride and groom from engagement to wedding day can be two very difference experiences. Ponder these questions for a reality check on the skills needed to work with a couple throughout the wedding process:

- Are you open-minded and willing to listen to other people's ideas when working on a project?
- Can you tactfully convince others of your point of view?
- Can you take someone's idea and make it even better by adding your own creative touches?
- Are you an out-of-the-box thinker, but tethered to the ground? Can you mix reality with a bit of fantasy?
- Are you organized? Methodical? A list maker?
- Can you multitask, or do you get nervous if one job is not complete before you start another?
- Is there a business side that balances your creative flair?
- Do you have negotiation skills?
- Are you willing to work weekends or evenings?
- Are you flexible, cooperative, understanding, and patient?
- Do you enjoy different personalities and perspectives?
- Are you both calm and energetic? Patient yet persistent? Cool under pressure and ready to move on to Plan B without a bead of sweat appearing on your brow?

If you can respond with an unflinching Yes to these questions, and feel ready to take on the myriad situations that would come your way as a wedding planner, you may be ready to try your hand at becoming a professional. If you are feeling a bit intimidated about the demands of being a wedding planner, don't fret. You can find support through training, hiring the right vendors, and joining professional organizations to help you round out your skills.

Recipe for Success

People skills come into play when you work with a couple to make their dreams a reality. Often you must temper their enthusiasm or encourage them to think outside of the box in order to create a unique wedding that captures their personal style. Organizational skills are important every step of the way as you juggle the couple, the wedding elements, and the vendors involved in the process. Part of being a professional involves keeping your eye on the end result while juggling the moving parts as you work toward the finish line. Many times you must reach out to a vendor or place an order and then wait for responses, confirmations, and deliveries. Business skills are needed to balance costs, your time, your client's budget, and the backup materials needed to keep all the aspects of the planning in order. After a day of client and vendor meetings, you may need to spend time at your computer, paying bills or sending invoices. Negotiation skills come into play from setting a price for your services to selecting vendors for your clients. You are constantly working to create a win-win for all parties and a dream wedding that is on budget, on time, and exactly what was ordered.

Are You Ready?

If you have realistically reflected on the personality style and skills needed to be a successful planner and feel it is a good fit for you, take a look at timing. Are you at a point in your life where you can make any necessary changes to start a business? Check out the list of questions presented and answer them before you journey forward. All of your responses will help you prepare to launch a successful wedding planning business.

Financing Your Venture

One important reason to start your own business is to reap financial rewards. But with this come responsibilities and risks. I will cover these issues in more detail in chapter 5, but you should at least think through how you will support yourself in the beginning stages and how you will fund some of the start-up costs. You may decide to start slowly and begin as a part-time consultant. One of the benefits of being a consultant is being in control of your company's growth. There are costs to starting some businesses that will require equipment, a storefront, and raw materials; not necessarily so for a home-based consultant's business. As a home-based wedding planner, you will be guiding couples through the planning process and taking tasks off their hands that they are unwilling, untrained, or too busy to do. Your greatest assets will be your time and talent. Once you identify what's needed to perform successfully, you can decide how much time you can—and want to—put into your new venture.

Getting the Know-How

So what makes you think you can do this job? Have you worked with a vendor for the wedding industry, such as a caterer or an event venue, or do you come from the hospitality field in another discipline? Are you transitioning from corporate or meeting planning in search of a more creative outlet for your skills? Have you just completed an undergraduate or graduate program and are looking for a job? No matter what your background is, it's a good idea to hone your skills in the specific area of wedding celebrations in order to be able to start and grow your business on a good foundation. Join a professional organization; volunteer or intern with a seasoned planner; consider taking some courses specific to the wedding industry. Check out chapter 12 for more details on education and training. There are trade shows and conferences with courses that will show you the intricacies of this specialized industry and help you to gain the knowledge and confidence necessary to plan to perfection.

Calling All Clients

Getting your first piece of business is usually easy. It may be what drives you to launch your business. It's getting the second and third client that's tricky. Word-of-mouth advertising, referrals, and networking are great, low-cost ways of marketing your business. Once you decide to formalize your company, you'll put the final polishing touches on the business with a catchy and professional name, business cards, and an informational Web site. There will be a gradual development of your marketing plan and your investment in promoting your business, but starting slowly and keeping your initial focus on professionalism is always a wise move.

The Right Ingredients

So, what does it really take? A good place to start would be to have the knowledge to get the job done, a great client, a strong contact list of vendors, and the time and energy to pull it all together. Does it take purchasing new equipment? Not unless you don't own a computer, printer, or phone. Does it take renting office space and hiring an administrative assistant? Not unless you have clients lined up outside your door and you don't have a corner available in your home to hold your necessary files and documents. Start small and build gradually to maximize your profits and assets.

Knowledge

While a sense of style and a love for the latest trends in weddings are important, an understanding of the planning basics is essential to launching a successful business. Training—whether it is a formal class or a course offered by a local chapter of the Association of Bridal Consultants (ABC) or International Special Events Society (ISES)—is always the first step. Internships or hands-on learning experiences are great, but the field has become much more complicated in recent years, requiring knowledge of planning tools and systems, resources for vendors, and a solid understanding of the legal implications to contracting on behalf of your client, as well as the liability exposures you may have. I will cover this in more detail in chapter 5 (Dollars and Sense) and chapter 12 (Being the Best). Consider completing a course or program of studies to start off on solid ground. I think anyone who is thinking about starting a business has to be an optimist by nature, but a dose of reality is important to keep both a business and a bank account in check. Remember: In order to charge a reasonable fee for your services, you must be worth the price. So, build your credentials first before promising something you cannot deliver.

Besides a basic knowledge of event coordination, you should also have a natural acumen for the activities that surround weddings. An eye for color and design, a sense of style for layout of your wedding space, and an understanding of music and entertainment will allow you to add value to the planning process. You must know how to source out the specific elements of the wedding process, such as invitations; favors; decor, including floral and linens; and vendors, such as photographers, videographers, and transportation companies. Building your "toolbox" and vendor list will come with time, but you should enjoy immersing yourself in these vital features of wedding planning right at the outset.

Business basics

Put aside your vision of a glamorous career in wedding planning and consider what goes on when the ballroom is cleared and the festivities have ended. There are bills to pay, invoices and thank-you notes to send, forms and evaluations to complete and mail. As a business owner you will be required to submit forms to your accountant and lawyer, state and federal agencies, and other services you may enlist to help keep your business healthy and profitable. You should have a basic understanding of software programs such as Microsoft Office to help develop your proposals, track expenses, and create planning worksheets. More sophisticated programs can help with floor plans and wedding checklists, as well as financial tracking of your business. Programs like QuickBooks or Quicken are often used by wedding planners, and can be easily integrated into the work done by a professional accountant later on, as your business grows. At first, you may have to bring yourself up to speed and handle the bookkeeping, report filing, and proposal duties yourself, in order to keep your expenses low and profits high.

The early stages of your business will require you to become familiar with many tasks that will ensure a successful life cycle for your company. It's also important to know how your business works so you can monitor your profit margin on jobs and know what is working and what is not. Especially in the early stages, you should know exactly how your company operates so you can maintain control of every aspect of the business, monitoring its progress and success. My father once shared a wise phrase with me: Inspect what you expect. This saying rings in my head when I work with vendors and contract labor for my events. It allows me to maintain a brand of excellence for my company, knowing that my mark is on the final product, even after many helping hands have made my vision come to life.

People skills

Wedding planning, which is part of the hospitality industry, is a "people" business. You must be able to get along and work with a variety of individuals, from clients and vendors to the staff that you hire and train. While you must have a strong sense of what your business stands for, your primary role is to fulfill the dreams of your clients and create the wedding they envision. This means you have to be flexible and cooperative as well as tactful and persuasive. Your ability to support the bride and groom with planning and industry knowledge will prove your value. Clients will look to you for advice, understanding, patience, and empathy. Emotions run high in this area of event planning, and you must be willing to ride the wave from the start of your relationship with your clients and their families to get a final product everyone is happy with.

Even before you land your first wedding client, you must be willing to "strut your stuff" and sell your services. Don't be afraid to tell family and friends about your dream of owning your own wedding planning business. If you are comfortable with your know-how, then talk it up. Share your ideas and become known as a wedding junkie. Be proud of your courage to try your hand at being an entrepreneur. You will have to continue to show your confidence at appointments with potential clients, at bridal fairs or expos, or when meeting venue staff to hand out your promotional materials. Don't confuse confidence and enthusiasm about your new business with bragging. Selling yourself is an essential part of growing your business. You need to be comfortable tooting your own horn if you want to successfully launch your business.

Vendors require another style of communication as you learn to negotiate pricing, develop contracts, and hold them to the bar of excellence you set. They, too, are often small business owners and have their own challenges when it comes to managing their success. Some vendors may overpromise, be disorganized, or not have your client at the top of their list. Managing their expectations as well as those of your clients can require a firm yet cooperative management style. I have had favorite vendors that could deliver the creative aspect of their service but lacked the ability to be on time and up-to-date with last-minute changes for the wedding. Evaluating and educating your service providers will ultimately allow you to put your best foot forward to your clients.

Wedding assistants, interns, or contract labor that you hire to assist you will need training and ongoing monitoring to ensure they deliver at the level you expect. It took me a long time to allow someone else to "run" a wedding on my behalf. It wasn't until I was certain that this person would interact with the client and vendors exactly as I would that I could comfortably step aside. You will probably be doing most of the work yourself at first, but if you are lucky enough to land a large wedding, you will definitely need help tying bows, setting up at the church, or putting final touches on the reception hall. My advice would be to spend time at the front end instructing helpers about the exact way you want them to perform, making frequent checks and adjustments to their work as you go along. The time you put in on the front end will pay off in the end. The last thing you want to do is re-tie 150 sashes because they were tied upside down or backward!

When to Start

When is it the right time to jump in, feet first? Consider your knowledge, your financial situation, and the time you have available to dedicate to launching and preparing for your business and clients. If you need to earn a set amount of money, then consider how feasible it is to quit your existing job. Consider taking on one client at a time while still juggling your current job. If you start slowly, you will have a financial cushion to support you during the start-up period.

If you are shy on know-how but heavy on enthusiasm for the industry, consider interning, volunteering, or working at a venue that specializes in weddings. Many venues have wedding consultants that serve as the main point person, guiding the brides and their families through the on-site planning process. While it wouldn't give you the experience with invitations or other vendors' services, it would give you a chance to delve into negotiations and contracting, and to observe firsthand a wedding celebration from start to finish.

Are you willing to take the time to start this exciting new career? Owning your own business is an all-consuming venture. It takes perseverance, hard work, a strong work ethic, and a positive attitude even in the face of adversity. It takes plenty of Plan B's to pull out of your hat when things don't go exactly as planned, remembering that most of the time, guests don't even realize that anything is wrong. At the end of the day, your true reward is the feeling you will have, knowing you've helped to create memories of a lifetime for the bride and groom and their family and friends.

Ready, Set, Plan

Whether you have been out of the workforce and for a while you're just reentering it, or you're fresh from college or transitioning from another job, ask yourself these questions:

Can I afford it?

Do I have the skills?

How will I get clients?

What will I need to make it work?

Am I ready to do it?

Nuts and Bolts

Today's wedding planner has many more details to manage than the bride of forty years ago who coordinated her own wedding. Supporting the celebration of marriage these days calls for experience with travel, understanding of more (and often complex) laws and contract regulations, and background knowledge of religious and cultural customs, as well as social trends and multiday activities surrounding the festivities of the celebration. Why? Because couples are busy, and more often than not, they are both working. The custom of celebrating weddings tends to withstand economic downturns, with wedding celebrations still being held even in a slow economy. With access to information and products from around the world and an awareness of celebrity weddings, the sky's the limit when it comes to what can be done in a wedding celebration. Time is at a premium for today's bride and groom, and they may be willing to pay for professional assistance to create the event of their dreams. They know what they want, and they also know the benefits of hiring a professional to help them achieve it.

Specialized Wedding Markets

Here are a few niche markets for wedding planners with a focus on unique wedding planning features and specialty areas:

Destination weddings

Religious specialties

Same-sex marriages

Events to support the wedding (showers, parties, favors, and travel/leisure)

According to The Wedding Report (www.theweddingreport.com), a company that provides information on wedding statistics and market research for the wedding industry, there were 2,308,000 celebrations in 2007. Wedding growth is expected to increase 8 percent each year. Of the more than two million weddings celebrated in 2007, 46 percent were paid for by the bride and groom, with most of the remaining weddings funded by either the bride or groom's family. The planning tools that the couple and their families drew on included bridal magazines, fairs, Internet resources, assistance from family and friends, and, of course, the professional wedding planner. According to the Bridal Association of America's (www.bridalassociationofamerica .com) "Wedding Report," more than 380,000 weddings were coordinated under the watchful eye of a wedding or bridal consultant. Are you ready to join the growing number and launch your own wedding planning business?

Do You Have What It Takes?

Take a look at some of the strengths you may need to have to succeed as a wedding planner, along with some weaknesses that could hinder you. Don't fret if you see some of your less-positive qualities on the list of weaknesses, as these can be turned around to good use in many instances.

Strengths

- Creative
- Articulate, good communicator
- Empathetic, good listener
- Sensitive and tactful
- Organized, with an ability to multitask
- Cool under pressure
- Hardworking and energetic
- Business-minded, financially knowledgeable

Weaknesses

- Willful—Turn this into a positive by being determined to make your business work!
- Unfamiliar with the wedding market—Start attending industry meetings and conferences and do some of your own research.
- Unsure of how much time you can give to your new venture—You can start with one wedding a week or one wedding a year; starting off slowly *is* a possibility.
- Like to have things go as planned—Being a planner is a positive, but as a wedding planner, you will want to be ready to go to Plan B when necessary.

How to Change Your Weaknesses into Strengths

If the list of weaknesses seems to describe some of your traits, consider your options to turn your dream of being a professional wedding planner into reality. If you are easily flustered, consider starting slowly until you build confidence. If you are a bit unsure about your potential success, think positively. Share your ideas with your friends and family and get their feedback. Like the children's book, *The Little Engine That Could,* imagine that you can achieve your dream, and work at turning your pessimism into optimism. Often it is mind over matter, and if you believe in your dream, and yourself, sooner or later it will come true! If you can't imagine listening to a bride describe her love for a certain shade of purple or why she wants to mix red and green on her Fourth of July wedding, stretch your comfort zone—because you will have to accommodate their vision for the wedding along with yours in order to create each couple's (not your own!) dream wedding. If you are unfamiliar with the wedding process, it would make sense to take courses, intern, or understudy before considering breaking out on your own. The field is exciting yet complex, and making a commitment to your first client requires solid knowledge for a successful outcome.

Work-Skill Assessment

Take this assessment to see how you can change your weaknesses into strengths.
1. How many years of experience do you have? If it's fewer than five, consider interning, working at a wedding facility, joining a professional organization for continuing education seminars, or registering for event-planning courses at a local college or university.
2. Are you willing and able to commit to starting your own business? If you are unsure about whether you have the time or energy, you may want to wait until your schedule is slower or you have a block of time to begin the necessary preparations. Consider starting slowly with one client and then growing your business slowly.
3. Are you sure you can handle an occasional "Bridezilla"? Take a deep breath and visualize the unhappy, nervous, uncompromising clients you may have. Visualize your responses to calm them down, negotiate for a win-win, and turn their feelings from stressed-out to stress-free . . . from overwhelmed to

overjoyed. You will have to look beyond the outward display of emotion and find out why the bride or her family reacts a certain way, and help to eliminate or reduce this stressor for a happy outcome.

4. Are you business- and event-savvy? Do you have skills in administration, marketing, sales, production, and event evaluation? If not, sign up for an event class and join your local event society or wedding association. Take evening classes in business topics or hire professionals to balance the areas you are deficient in. You won't have a budget for many employees at the beginning, so the more you can take on yourself, the easier it will be for your bottom line.

5. When will the time be right? Are you busy with your current job or family obligations? Do you have the space in your home to set up a small office? Make a plan to get your surroundings ready before the first couple comes your way. While it doesn't take a large office or lots of equipment, it will take a commitment to organizing your space and schedule to keep the necessary planning process orderly for your clients, right from the start.

What to Consider Before Taking the Leap

While there are many questions to ask yourself before taking the plunge into business ownership, first and foremost you must have a burning desire to own your own wedding planning company. It will be hard work, require long hours, and sometimes be frustrating, but it can also be lots of fun. Owning your own business gives you the flexibility to work when and how long you want. You are able to incorporate personal goals and activities into your day. You can spend the wee hours of the morning on production schedules and timelines and run to a 9:30 am Zumba class at the gym. Your schedule is your own, although there will be plenty of weekend work in your future as a wedding planner. You can choose to focus on one client a month, or five. You can also decide to add assistants or other levels of service such as invitations and favors to your offerings. Being the boss lets you choose when and how you will grow your business and what that business will be. There can be financial and personal rewards depending on how dedicated you are to growing your business and managing it in a professional way.

Along with the benefits of being self-employed come challenges. Take a look at the areas you will need to be cautious about when launching your wedding planning business:

Training

Make sure you take a few courses, understudy with a pro, and start small. Don't take on a 400-person tented wedding for your first project without understanding the implications of tent erection, lighting, electrical, and power needs. Take baby steps as you proceed, and don't begin until you have the confidence to do the job right. This will help you create weddings that are successes from the very start.

Time Management

Launching a business is time-consuming. It's best to do it properly from the beginning. Cutting corners by not having an official company name or business cards will make you look unprofessional and will not inspire the confidence you need with your clients. Before the first strains of "Here Comes the Bride" are heard, there are countless business details to attend to. These can be done in the evenings if you are still working elsewhere, or on your days off. To ensure that you are viewed as a professional, it is best to take as long as necessary to arrange the business matters of your new company so you can start off on the right foot. You may have to give something else up, such as a volunteer project or leisure activity, to fit all the details into each day, but this is the sacrifice you must make to achieve your goal.

Business-Savvy

Business skills will be just as important to the health of your new company as planning skills. You should fill in the gaps with classes or tutorials on the basic knowledge that will allow you to run your company professionally, such as computer skills and financial/accounting know-how. You should familiarize yourself with networking groups that are in your area to help you get new leads or contacts with possible vendors or suppliers. You will also need to seek advice from legal and financial experts who often participate in these networking groups. This may require extra time in the evenings, but it will be well worth the effort in the long run.

Reality Check

Optimism can be a double-edged sword. You have to be an optimist to believe in yourself and think you can make this work, but you also have to have a touch of reality in the equation. Don't overcommit or overpromise. Don't overbook clients or underestimate how long things will take. Temper your excitement for your new venture to eliminate painful learning experiences that will spoil the fun of starting your own business. Leave time in your day to answer phone calls, send out invoices, or write checks to suppliers. Don't forget your other responsibilities to family, friends, or your personal health. Maintaining a balance in your life is important in order to keep the stress levels down and your business and your mental state healthy.

Making Money

Being paid for your time is one of the pluses of owning a business. Once you have the training and are ready to launch your business, don't forget to charge for your services—and make sure you get paid. While you are in training, you may opt either to help a friend or to intern for a seasoned planner. This is volunteer time well spent. But when you actually begin your business, don't forget to record your time and charge accordingly. Keep track of appointments with both clients and vendors, trips to the floral supply warehouse, and time spent drafting copy for invitations and researching catchy ways to create save-the-dates and favors, such as photo magnets or green-theme take-aways. You will want to be recognized as being worth the investment, so set a reasonable price and deliver to satisfy. I will cover pricing your services in more detail in Chapter 5.

Picking and Choosing

It's exciting to get your first client, but knowing when to walk away from a project and when to say "I do" is important. I often get calls from people inquiring about my services and my fees. They will try to negotiate a minimum price to meet their budget while still getting the services they need to make their special day run smoothly. Unless it is a good friend or you can see additional business opportunities coming from this event in the future, it's always best to stick to your guns. Set a minimum fee for day or hourly services and hold to your pricing. Chapter 5 has ideas on how to present your services and be compensated fairly for the work you do. If you take business that doesn't pay, you end up feeling resentful and not wanting to put in the 100 percent that is necessary to make both you and the client happy.

Hobby vs. Job

Planning a wedding is fun! You wouldn't be considering this career if you didn't think you would enjoy it. But opening your own business specializing in wedding planning comes with responsibilities—to clients, vendors, assistants, and to yourself. You need to take every step of the process seriously as you purchase materials for clients, contract with venues to hold your events, and commit to the time necessary to get the job done. When you start your company, you cross the line between doing something just for fun and having to carry your commitments to fruition. It takes stamina, follow-through, and perseverance. And during the process there is a financial responsibility assumed by both your client and you, as a planner, to fulfill your end of the bargain. This commitment will take time and energy . . . sometimes when you least have it.

Top Ten Reasons to Take the Leap

1. You can't picture yourself doing anything else.
2. You have every wedding magazine available and have read them cover to cover.
3. You have watched *The Wedding Planner* at least twenty times.
4. You get calls from family and friends asking how to put the finishing touches on their celebrations.
5. You have been spending more time watching TV programs on weddings than working.
6. You have a burning desire to throw rice . . . just because.
7. You have enrolled in a butterfly release course, just so you have it in your bag of tricks.
8. You stop your car when you see a wedding being celebrated.
9. Your job would be more than just "work"—it would be fun and exciting, and a way to help others—and it would be your very own!
10. You can't picture yourself not helping a bride to make her wedding day picture-perfect!

Top Ten Mistakes

1. Treating your new business as a hobby.
2. Not taking the time to listen to your clients' concerns or complaints.
3. Not following your instincts.
4. Not spending the necessary time "detailing" your business.
5. Charging too little.
6. Charging too much.
7. Not getting the right (or enough) training.
8. Trying to do it all yourself.
9. Not taking any time for yourself.
10. Not taking a chance.

Frequently Asked Questions

1. *I am graduating from college and want to start my own business. Will brides be willing to hire someone who may seem young and inexperienced?*
   The best way to get hired is to begin as an apprentice with a more-experienced planner. The early stages of a client relationship may include an initial meeting where you serve as an assistant to the seasoned planner. As the planning progresses, you will have the opportunity to show your value as you offer advice and take care of the countless details involved in the planning process. This is a great way to get a handle on the process while being under the watchful eye of a pro.

2. *I am a teacher; could I run a wedding planning business as a second job, seeing that I have weekends and summers off? Is it even possible to juggle this new venture with an already-existing job?*
   It's not only possible but advisable to consider another plan for income when you are just starting off in the wedding planning industry. You will want to have some financial support, whether it comes from another job, a loan, or a partner who helps with your living expenses while you get your company off the ground. Meetings with vendors and clients can be worked around a light or part-time day schedule. Weddings are often on weekends,

when a typical Monday-through-Friday job would not interfere. Consider easing into your new business to keep your stress level down, at least when it comes to finances.

3. *I just helped plan my sister's wedding and it was a great experience. How can I get my feet wet in the industry?*

    Consider approaching a church and asking if they have a day-of-event coordinator on staff. It may be a paid or volunteer job, but it will get you in the wedding mode quickly. Or, contact an established planner and ask if he or she needs help with setup on wedding days. Most planners would love to have an able and willing person who is passionate about the industry assisting them; a person who will treat the wedding process with the attention for detail that is necessary. Even if you aren't paid for some early projects, it will give you the experience you need to launch your company.

4. *Are wedding consultants in demand today? Is it a growing industry?*

    While many industries go through slumps from time to time, for special event planners, the wedding market tends to remain consistent. Even if the economy takes a dip, weddings will still be celebrated and busy people will still call on professionals for advice and assistance. While budgets may be smaller, wedding planners can add value by offering ways to cut costs and still get a memorable wedding day. People still believe in the institution of marriage and celebrate this custom with a festive affair. With couples approaching their nuptials at a later age, both often employed and busy, hiring a wedding planner is a must! Destination and multicultural weddings have also become increasingly popular options for a specialized segment of the wedding planning industry, adding to the demand for experienced planners.

For a wedding consultant, an office in the home is a very reasonable location in which to begin your business endeavor. Most often the face-to-face meetings with clients and vendors can be conducted outside the wedding planner's office, making a home-based office perfect for running the behind-the-scenes details. Selecting linens can be done at your rental company's showroom, food tastings sampled at the caterer's office, and discussions with the bride concerning invitations and time lines can be taken care of at a local hotel or restaurant. Once you develop a list of venues you would like to work with, most catering or event managers would be happy to have you bring a bride in to discuss the planning details, giving them the opportunity to showcase their property. They may even treat you to coffee and dessert as an extra perk!

Designing Your Space

When you are not conducting meetings and site inspections, you will need a spot to take care of the business details of your new venture. To begin with, you will need the bare minimum of space and supplies. A small room that can be converted into an office is ideal. This can be a spare bedroom, a study, a den, or even a corner of your basement. If you are handy or know of a good carpenter, consider partitioning off a part of the basement with drywall to give the space a formal feel. For the finishing touches, try jazzing up the walls with some fresh paint, adding the office essentials, such as a desk, chair, worktable, file cabinets, and lighting, and voilà! You have your own private area to launch your new business.

If you don't have access to a full room, section off part of a larger room with a wooden screen or by arranging furniture to create a separate space. This is doable if you live alone and can manage the surrounding area by keeping the two spaces separate. While not ideal, at least you will have a formal spot for filing and storage, and a place to go when you are in "work" mode. If you don't have an area you can close off, just make sure it is private enough for quiet conversations when a business call comes in. Setting the professional tone from the start is important, and that means limiting extraneous sounds like the television, family chatter, or crying babies.

While we are thinking about setting up your work space, consider your own style when you are in your home. Are you the type who has a hard time walking away from a sink full of dishes or a pile of laundry waiting to be washed? If so, set up some systems that will help you focus on work while you are in your home; this may be as simple as creating a list every morning that prioritizes your day. To succeed in your home office, you will have to treat your work life differently than your home life. (I will cover work/life balance in more detail in chapter 3.) This means that when you step into your "office space"—whether it's a room with a door you can close or a corner that houses your desk and files—you know it's time to focus on getting the job done. It will take discipline not to be distracted by the many other things that you might consider doing in your home instead of moving your business forward.

To operate a business successfully, there are a few staples to consider when setting up the elements of your home office:

Basic Equipment

To start off, a desk, chair, filing system, worktable, and bookcase will do the trick. You may even cut costs by using a nicely trimmed and painted piece of plywood over two filing cabinets for an extra large desk and work area. Add some shelving and either drawers or storage containers, and you are good to go! Make your office space an area you want to go to. Don't forget lighting and room decor, such as an attractive lamp, some photos, or a wall print. Select containers made of materials that reflect your style and will help you to keep things in order. Stylish baskets, plastic bins, or wooden boxes are available from local department stores or online, and offer an inexpensive way to keep things tidy and organized. Keep things simple and neat and provide sufficient places to file and store. As you develop your vendor list and gather samples to show your brides, you will want them handy and accessible when you need them, but tucked neatly away when not in use.

Technology

Top your desk with a laptop or desktop computer, a phone/fax combination, and a printer/scanner. These few pieces will give you what you need to get started. There are many choices to make in selecting your equipment. A laptop will give you portability, but is typically more expensive. If you think you will be presenting to clients off-site and using your computer to do so, go for a laptop. In terms of printers, inkjet will be less expensive than laser. You can find color printers with a copy/scanner option for the most efficient use of space and resources. If you think you will be printing items for your clients in large quantities, you may decide to invest in a good laser printer, as they are typically faster and offer better quality. A good digital camera has become a must-have to capture your successes and help you to develop marketing materials. To complete your technological tool kit, you may want to add a PDA (personal digital assistant) such as a Palm Pilot, or a phone/PDA combination like the iPhone to keep track of contacts and appointments, and also allow you to take photographs to save and send to clients. If these don't fit into your start-up budget, a simple calendar with a jazzy cover will fit the bill just fine!

Software Must-Haves

To manage the business details of your business you will need basic word processing and spreadsheet capabilities. You will be writing letters, developing proposals and marketing materials, keeping track of guest lists, and creating budgets. Microsoft Office offers suites in various levels that range from Basic to Enterprise editions. The Small Business edition offers accounting, marketing, and publishing tools for one-stop shopping, which can help in various areas of your business. You may not have to develop detailed PowerPoint presentations, but you may decide to dabble in Publisher if you want to create marketing or business communication materials. A stand-alone accounting program such as QuickBooks (Intuit) is widely used by professional accountants and may make tax time easier. Check with your accountant ahead of time for a recommendation before investing in a program that may not integrate with his or her services.

As you advance in your business, you may want to catalog wedding photos or create slide shows to present to prospective clients or vendors. Unless you have a natural knack or understanding of computer technology, it can be time-consuming to develop this skill for your business. There are some simple movie programs that come with many of the office packages that will allow you to complement your photographs with music and text to showcase your work in a professional way. Another option for creating this type of marketing piece is to find a good vendor who will help you create it (with the added benefit of being able to recommend this vendor for video work with your clients).

Another software add-on for the computer-savvy would be Microsoft FrontPage. This program allows you to build your own company Web site and update it as often as you wish. You can change your home page and add photos or text as you gather experience and add successful weddings to your portfolio. If you are high on technological savvy but low on start-up funds, this could be an option for building and maintaining your own Web site without the expense of a professional webmaster. Other options for Web site development will be covered in chapter 11 (E-Commerce and Internet Use).

Business Supplies

Once you decide on your company's name, you will need business cards, letterhead, checks, and deposit slips to support your business transactions. You may decide to get a stamp with your deposit information, or choose to print personalized notes to include with correspondence you have with clients and vendors. While all of this will look nice, it's not imperative to have at the beginning. You could even print your company name directly from your computer onto festive paper before making the investment with a professional print shop for a full letterhead and envelope set. You will have many choices on how to set up your company professionally. My advice is to begin with the bare minimum that will let you start off in a professional manner, and then build as your income increases.

Client Binders

Most of my client details are logged immediately into a three-ring binder with section tabs for the various elements of the wedding. All correspondence, contracts, forms, and planning details can be organized in this one location. A binder with a clear front and side will allow you to create a personal cover for each wedding. Clear sleeves allow for small or unusually shaped items to be kept in the binder. A front business card sheet keeps the various vendor cards easy to assess and in one spot.

Other ways to organize your client information may be in file folders, accordion filing containers, or electronically, on your computer. (If you prefer the latter, don't forget to make hard copies or back up all digital information as a precaution in case you have a system crash or the electricity isn't working and you need quick access to the information.)

Proposals and Marketing Materials

Some of the items listed in the office basics chart that follows will cover your needs for typical tasks, but you might consider adding specialty papers for proposals, tools such as grommet makers, and festive edgers or hole punches to put a creative touch on your work. A binding machine will also allow you to create proposals that look professional and customize the covers to reflect your style and brand. You can use a clear cover and add your special touch to each page to get the look you want.

Specialty Planning Tools

To complement a basic office software suite, you may consider using specialty software unique to the wedding industry, such as iDo Wedding and Event Professional Edition software or Event Magic Pro, which offer options for contracting, budgeting, guest list management, and seating charts. There are other planning tools available that can be helpful in keeping things organized. While you may be able to rely on the venue or tent company to provide diagrams and room layouts, it is always a good idea to become familiar with drawing your own in either Word or PowerPoint.

Office Basics

Equipment	Technology	Software	Supplies
Desk	Cell Phone	Office Suite	Paper: plain/ specialty
Chair	Phone	Accounting	Scissors/Hole Punch/Stapler
Worktable	Fax	Presentation	Paper Clips/ Grommets
File Cabinet(s)	Printer	Label Maker	Labels/Stickers
Lamp	Scanner	Photo	3-Ring Binders/ Tabs
Storage Containers	Digital Camera	Movie Maker	Plastic Sleeves
Bookshelves	CD Player	CD Burner	Notepads/ Post-its®

Even basic programs such as these will have shapes and line functions to help you to create tables, staging, and walkways as part of a Word document. Make sure you keep things to scale so you don't end up not having enough room or misjudging how much space you have.

What It Costs

Setting Up an Office

Printer/fax/scanner: $49.99 for a basic model to $375 or more for lots of fancy features

Digital camera-megapixel digital camera with zoom: $79.99 to $600 (video camera capabilities)

Event-planning software: $99

Hands-free headset: $20 to $100

Two-way radios/walkie-talkies: $15 to $100

GPS navigational system: $150 to $1,000+ (but could be up to $2,000)

Smartphone / PDA / BlackBerry (with e-mail and Web capabilities): $150 (with rebates) to $750+

Small business high-speed Internet packages: as low as $39.99/month with rebates

File cabinets: $150

Desks: from $150

Comfortable chair: $60 to $170

Wedding Resources

While many home-based businesses require specialized equipment, a wedding planner has a unique mix of essentials in his or her bag of tricks. You may have invitation samples, ribbons and lace, and a book of names including your favorite calligrapher, florist, and photographer. To enhance the basic office, you will also begin to acquire decorative items that help you in your business. I have collected a supply of votive candle holders, vases and urns, and ribbons, all of which are easily reused. My storage tripled after an addition to our home, and I have happily taken over one stall of our three-car garage to store these items. I feel fortunate to have this additional space, but it took many years in business to get to this point. Unless you have a large storage area, you may want to keep your incidental supplies to a minimum—but there are a few items you bring along with you on event day.

Some of the essentials for an on-site wedding toolbox would include materials to help mend or repair decor, pins and fasteners to assist the bride or attendants, or personal or safety items to attend to any small needs. Don't assume the role of nurse or doctor if an emergency arises, but if a tissue or Band-Aid is needed or bug spray is requested, it's handy to have it on hand.

Creativity Basics to Have in Your Home-Based Business

Specialty papers: paper and stationery samples, catalogs, and order binders for stationery products

Craft products: ribbons, ribbon cutter, specialty scissors, pearl-topped pins, needles, and thread

Art and decor items: candles, mirror rounds, vases, holders, frames (for table numbers or signs)

Specialty vendors/products: stationery vendors such as Carlson Craft or planning software such as iDo Wedding and Event Professional Edition

Other helpful items might include personal care essentials for a frazzled wedding party member, such as bottled water, candy or mints, antiperspirant towelettes, or lollipops, or crucial items for guests or vendors, like tape, paper, pens, batteries (AA or AAA), or an extension cord. While you don't have to be able to provide everything asked for, you will come out looking like a star if you can solve a last-minute problem.

If the reception will be held at a hotel or club, you are more likely to have access to things like extension cords or basic stationery items like pens, paper, or pins. If your wedding is an outside event or a tented affair, you should plan to have any last-minute tools to fix swags that are drooping or chair covers that have torn. (See the Event Supplies and On-Site Wedding Toolbox sidebars for a more complete list of items.)

Event Supplies

- Hammer
- Nails
- Zip ties
- Glue gun and glue sticks
- Pins
- Pushpins or tacks
- Clips
- Roping: string, thread, twine

On-Site Wedding Toolbox

- Ribbon: white/wedding color
- Pins: safety, pearl-topped, common, T-pins
- Stationery: pens, paper, tape, paper clips, scissors, glue stick
- Hardware: extension cords, glue gun, stapler, zip ties
- Floral: wire, ties, tape
- Personal items: antiperspirant wipes, mints or throat lozenges, aspirin or ibuprofen, small water bottles, personal tissue packs, bug spray

Your Home Environment

Deciding to set up a home-based business may affect more than just your clients and your own personal space. Depending on your living situation, you may be moving someone out of a room to get your own office, or sharing a space with other family members or roommates. You may have to consider the sound impact from visitors or other family members or housemates. It will be important to count on having time in your office that is uninterrupted, and an environment that is quiet enough to allow you to conduct your business in a professional manner.

A running joke in our family had to do with the rules that I had for my children while they were growing up. They have always lived in a home with a working mom who had a home office. My rules, called the "Three Bs," were quite simple: When I was in my office, the kids were not to disturb me unless someone was bleeding or not breathing or something was burning. Two emergencies did pull me from my phone—once, when my neighbor's house caught fire, and another time when a skateboarding jump didn't work out for my son's friend and we had to rush him to the emergency room. The moral of this story: Set parameters that everyone can live with, and don't be afraid to enforce them.

Frequently Asked Questions

1. *Business software seems very expensive. Do I need event-planning software right away, or should I wait until I have multiple clients?*
   To get your business off to a professional start, I would recommend a basic office suite that, at the very least, includes word processing for letters, proposals, invitations, and menu cards, and a spreadsheet program for budgets, lists, and charts. (You can add to this with specialized software for wedding planners as you grow.) Doing things from scratch will help you develop some basic skills to keep your business and your clients organized and to help you understand the basic steps of your wedding planning business.
   If you don't want to invest in financial software, you could create your invoices in Excel, but as soon as you can, it would be worth streamlining things and moving to a program that interacts with online banking and your receivables and invoices.

2. *How do I separate my household to-do lists from my wedding planning to-do lists?*

While lists are important, too many lists can be overwhelming. Since you are ultimately responsible for being at every business appointment or lacrosse game, a master appointment schedule is the way to go. To complement your appointment book or Outlook calendar, to-do lists will keep you on track to get things done on time. Too many items on your lists can be difficult to manage, so consider grouping them by clients or projects. I am not advocating leaving out details—in this business, it is important to remember even the smallest task—but to organize them in a manageable fashion. I recommend having a notebook or computer document that you can use to create your to-do list, which can be updated daily or weekly. Take a look at the sidebar for a typical to-do list that I have created (see page 32).

I also have a notebook by my bed that I use to jot down things that I need to get done the next day; by writing them down, I can put them out of my head and get a good night's rest. I also have small notebooks handy in my car and purse for phone messages or things I don't want to forget; I jot them down and transfer them later to my master to-do list. For your home tasks, consider using a corkboard or message area to enlist the help of other family members in getting things done, thereby removing some of the burden from your shoulders.

3. *I don't know any specialty vendors. How do you compile and build a list of vendors/resources?*

The best way to find good vendors is to ask someone who has used them. If you can put together a networking group to share ideas and issues, you will learn who your colleagues are using and who they have had success or problems with. If you join an industry group such as the International Special Events Society (ISES) or the Association of Bridal Consultants (ABC), you will have access to monthly meetings and wedding professionals who attend meetings and are members. These are great resources for building your little red book of names and contacts. Don't be afraid to ask hotels or country clubs you visit who they have had success with. They will be happy to share their top picks for florals, photography, or limousine services.

4. *How many clients should I take on in my first year?*

Depending on how much time you have and whether you will start your business full-time or ease into it will determine how much you can take on at the start. My advice would be to apprentice with an experienced planner at the outset, and also offer to help a close friend or family member with his or her nuptials. Start with a smaller wedding with traditional details and ease into the destination or multicultural affairs. During high wedding season (spring and fall), you could end up with a wedding each weekend, but I wouldn't take on more than two per month to start with. Once you get your planning time lines established and resources lined up, you can take on more as you feel comfortable. At the beginning, you will be doing most of the planning, meeting, and legwork yourself, so make sure you allot sufficient quality time for all of your clients.

The Balancing Act

Starting your own business will bring unique challenges to both your work and family life. As an employee, you typically will have set work hours, a predetermined salary or hourly rate, and days off each week or for special holidays. As a self-employed wedding planner, you will drive your daily schedule, your workload, and how many hours you work and play. Ultimately, only you will be responsible for getting the job done and building your reputation as a reliable, professional, and organized wedding planner. With this new responsibility for your business and clients comes choosing how you will allot your time to make it all happen!

Planning Your Schedule

Consider your day a pie chart, divided up into slices. Each activity in the day will use a percentage of that precious twenty-four-hour pie that represents your life. How will you slice it? Can you afford to put all your eggs into the work basket and risk earning the reputation of a workaholic? Can you streamline some portions of your life and bow out of commitments that you have had in the past that you may have to give up in order to assume your new role as business owner? There is no need to make excuses for saying no; you have a great reason to make this commitment. You are starting your own business!

Prioritizing

Start by dividing up your values into sections. Work, family, self, volunteering, and basic routines are all possible categories. How will you portion your twenty-four-hour day? Take a look at the sidebar for a glimpse at how I typically prioritize my monthly schedule. I have a family and pets, I'm active in my church, and I'm beginning to focus on the care of my mother, who lives out of state. While it is easy to focus on just one or two areas, such as work and self, we often have to consider our family, friends, or community as we go about our daily lives. Be honest with what you are willing to give up for your new venture.

Weekly Commitments

Work: Ongoing projects, marketing for new business, training interns. Daily: 10 hours.

Professional: Attend meetings 2x per month, read industry e-mails and journals. Weekly: 6 hours.

Family: Attend sporting events, chauffeur to activities, manage meals, shopping, oversee and delegate household chores such as laundry, cleaning, yard work, pet care, family chat time. Daily: 3 hours.

Self: Work out. Daily: 1 hour.

Friends: Quick glass of wine with a friend, couples' dinner, book group, Zumba class. Weekly: 2 hours.

Volunteering: Attend planning meeting for art gallery gala, rehearsals for youth choir, mentor high school student. Weekly: 5 hours.

Routine Activities: Sleep, eat, bathe. Daily: 9 hours.

Work Time

Starting your own business will take an incredible amount of time and effort. When jobs roll in, you will have to fit them into an already-busy schedule. It feels like I spend all of my waking hours thinking about work: projects that are in place, new business, vendors, clients, and the business of special events in general. I constantly think of new ways to use things I see in shops and on walks. I typically will go to my office after dinner and finish up planning schedules, e-mails, or client correspondence. I often make calls to clients in the evening, after the traditional workday, when it is more convenient for them to discuss their wedding plans. Because you have to be "on call" for clients when needed, consider making your schedule guilt-free to suit your needs. The beauty of having your own business is having time to work out in the middle of the morning if you want to—or to volunteer in your child's classroom during the week, knowing that you will have to work on the weekend for a bride. Take advantage of the flexibility of your schedule and take some time for yourself when you can squeeze it in.

Sample of Weekly To-Do Lists

Here is a sampling of what tasks you would need to juggle if you had two weddings on your schedule. Consider how you would get them done, what support you'd need, and how it would fit into your day or week.

Shannon and Donald

- Check on other locations
- Reorder RSVP card
- Check on butterflies with Jodi
- Look for cages for ceiling of Loggia
- Get more grapevine nests to hang; look in floral supply store for nests and additional silk butterflies to enhance décor.
- Send check for transportation
- List music for church and copy and send in mail; copy and e-mail to Sherry
- Find Siena's contract
- Order votives (ivory, straw, sterling, honeydew, and pastel yellow)
- Get permit from town for indoor candles; call fire department
- Get permit for draping; bring sample and forms and votives
- Guestbook: reorder (did 3/30)
- Call caterer with numbers
- Cake (tell we have topper, may have 140 people, work with florist)
- Decide on ribbons
- Order butterfly reception cards
- Order table cards
- Get candy bags
- Get runner
- Order program booklet

Lauren and Rob

- Confirm transportation, print orders, and check against our schedule
- Confirm linens; add the cake table; call CE Rentals and ask what would be good
- E-mail Mary re: flowers and centerpieces; e-mail photos FYI and schedule
- Develop chair cover, but wait as they may be getting cream ones; order when confirmed
- Cut the stickers and send to Jane
- Check on venue: order chardonnay, pinot grigio, merlot choices to be passed as well as Heineken and light beer (very cold)
- Confirm staffing four bartenders all the time; double bar in Colonnade, double bar in cocktail area (two); bar closes during dinner, then move one bartender inside room and keep two bartenders outside room; CHECK WITH JANE
- Confirm final numbers three days out (as of 4/1): brunch: 135, dinner: 173
- Decrease napkin count, 60-inch rounds, feed eight per table
- Order cake linen: Mazzotti polka cream
- Bring pink votives and use with inn's white ones
- Wine: pinot grigio ($2 pp upgrade) ($116 total); Stella Chardonnay Domain Bernier; merlot: Maison Nicolas Reserve; beer: Heineken, Miller Light (at bar)
- Use inn's cocktail napkins

Family Time

Just because you are passionate about your new business venture doesn't mean your loved ones will feel the same way. Depending on your marital status, whether you have children (and their ages), and other family commitments, such as caring for siblings or parents, you will have to be clear with your loved ones about abiding by the schedule you will need to follow in order to get your business launched.

Consider starting with a family meeting and laying out a chart of chores, schedules, and commitments. Unless you do this, you may be simply adding to your workload without getting the support you need. You may be pleasantly surprised at how willing your loved ones will be to pitch in for the benefit of all. The end result can be additional income from you, less stress with a shared workload in the home, and a feeling of empowerment as the household contributes to a team effort. Don't forget to recognize the additional effort put forth with verbal praise and an occasional treat!

If you live alone, you have the luxury of not having to worry about family commitments, but also the sole responsibility and burden of doing household chores by yourself or enlisting paid services to help you. You may also want to take time for friends or social groups so your life doesn't become lopsided as you schedule your daily activities.

Family Balance

Although my children are rapidly becoming adults, they are still such an important part of my life. My husband also has a home-based business, so we have the luxury of touching base during the day as officemates. I have been able to group some of my activities together to maximize my time. For instance, my daughter Kate and I make a date to attend several exercise classes together each week. We have discovered Zumba at our local gym and have even included some event colleagues and clients into our passion for this fun way to workout and reenergize. When our schedules don't allow for a commitment to a class, I switch workout partners and join my husband for a treadmill chat.

We still try to eat together as a family, something we have always done despite our crazy schedules. Dinnertime also gives us a chance to chat with our son Kevin and stay tuned into his life as a freshman at a local university. There are many basic tasks like chauffeuring and shopping that are shared in our family, taking the pressure off. My husband typically takes the 4:30 am hockey practice run for our youngest daughter, Paige, but I still try to attend all the hockey and lacrosse games. By combining exercise time with family time and adding friends and clients into the daily routine, I really maximize my time!

Time for Yourself

If you are passionate about the field of wedding planning, it doesn't seem like a burden to be eating, living, and breathing your job. Who wouldn't want to have a job they love! The risk of not stepping away from work is that you don't open yourself up to new ideas, to meet new people outside of the industry, or to give yourself a break. Even if you don't think you need it, stepping away from your clients will give you a fresh perspective. It may seem provincial to put clothes out on a line, but I love to hang a batch of towels out to dry. The fifteen minutes it takes allows me time to think and enjoy the quiet of the morning. Stepping away from the phone and frenzy of work gives me renewed energy to face my busy day. If you don't classify yourself as the "spiritual" type, even this simple quiet time can give you the centering you may need. Whether you choose to attend mass or synagogue, take a yoga class or meditate, your spiritual health deserves a slice in your "time pie."

Take a little time to pamper yourself, too: get your nails done, go shopping or to the library. Consider hiring a house cleaner or yard service to free you up to enjoy time on your own. You may prefer to do some chores yourself, like gardening or organizing the garage. Consider these "chores" personal time worth taking, to kill two birds with one stone. Take a moment every month to reward yourself for stepping out with your new business, and you will end up healthier and more balanced in the long run, returning to your clients refreshed and ready to take on their challenges.

Above all, don't ignore your body's health. Watch your diet and get plenty of exercise. Inactivity and eating on the run will soon take its toll on your persona as a true professional. So add the trip to the gym into your day planner and hit the road when the alarm goes off. Try scheduling self-care first thing in the day, so you don't end up running out of time and not fitting it in day after day. Consider a delivery service for groceries or a prepackaged meal service to make sure you get what you need, when you need it.

Friends

Adding time for contact with kindred spirits can do a world of good for our psyche. Friends can offer a change of perspective, sound advice, or a soft shoulder to lean on. They can also be a great source of leads and referrals. You will undoubtedly create industry friends with whom you can commiserate and discuss work challenges. You may also have friends who have nothing to do with the events or wedding industry and simply give you a change of scenery when you spend time together. Even though there are only twenty-four hours in a day, consider combining time with friends as part of your nonwork activities, such as exercise or volunteerism, to keep your life full and your stress level down.

Volunteering

Church, cultural, or philanthropic activities can all add a sense of balance to a busy person's life. Even though you may want to put all your focus on your new business, the break you take to go meditate, attend a religious service, or volunteer for a fund-raising event can help take the edge off your busy life. Consider choosing activities that you love, are good at, or will give you more time with family or friends. You may even find you can gain experience and contacts by helping out at a community or school event, indirectly benefiting your business in the long run. Plus, you will feel better about yourself and return to your clients with a fresh outlook.

Other Commitments

If you are lucky enough to own your own home and not have many other responsibilities on your plate, the sky's the limit on how you spend your time and organize your space. Most of us don't have that luxury and must take into consideration daily responsibilities such as child care, parental care, volunteer commitments, home and family duties—just to name a few. Setting up an office in your home may intrude upon other people's space. My advice would be to be firm, honest, and open about what you need to make it work. It will be important to have support from most of the people who are affected by your decision to start your own business. Your loved ones should be proud and encourage you to move forward with your dream. When it begins to cut into their space, it becomes more difficult, and that's when the cooperation between parties begins. Don't be afraid to regroup and redefine your needs. You will need to stand firm to get the space and time needed to make your new venture work.

Child-Care Options

If you have a family, setting a professional tone for your home-based business will be essential. Set limits from the start. If you have small children, designate time in your office that is quiet and undisturbed. To set and maintain a professional appearance, you should limit or eliminate extraneous background noises that would make your clients feel as though you were distracted. The most convenient situation would be finding care for them in an off-site setting, such as a nursery school or day-care center or in a private home. Although it is hard to see your little ones leave you, if you are ready and willing to start your business, you should plan for child care that will benefit both you and your child. If you are trying to multitask by juggling both the attention of your business and your children, one or both parties will suffer. But if your children are in off-site care, they will benefit from playing with others and having their needs attended to promptly, and your clients will benefit from having your undivided attention as well. It can be a win-win situation, if you find the right out-of-home child-care provider. Consider flexibility (you may not need a full-time commitment), pricing (evaluate hourly rates, partial week programs, or drop-in centers), environment (other children to play with, outside and inside playtime, healthy snacks, and a setting you are comfortable with), and convenience (location nearby, car pooling with friends or neighbors, or pickup options).

When I first started my business, I ran to the phone and computer as soon as naptime hit and was able to get quite a bit done. When I had appointments or deadlines that were looming, my mother-in-law and a trusted local mom happily took care of my little one. As my family and my business grew, more formal child-care arrangements became a necessity. As my children entered school, I could depend on a 9–3 workday without the expense of child care. My mom filled in to provide full-time care when travel took me away from home. I also benefited from having her prepare dinners, iron dress shirts, and vacuum the floors. (An au pair or live-in nanny can provide a similar service, but not at the price that my mom charged!) There are

Some Costs

In-home child care	$10 to $25 per hour based on experience
Day-care center	$100 to $400 per week depending on time and number of children
Live-in nanny	$100 to $300 per week
House cleaner	$80+ depending on tasks and frequency of use
Spa experience	$100 to $1,500+ depending on treatments, services, and length of stay
Membership at gym	$20 to $100 per month
Manicure and pedicure	$15 to $100
Dinner and a movie	$50+

many reliable companies worldwide that can provide local or international staff, both male and female. Hiring a "manny" (a male version of a nanny) has become more popular for families with boys, as they often share similar interests and have a more comfortable relationship with the children.

Defining Your Support Needs

Whether you decide to hire an in-home babysitter or bring your child off-site, it is important to decide on the level of support you need and communicate it clearly. If you can hire someone who can help out with light cleaning or food preparation while the kids are napping, it will make the end of the day run more smoothly for you. If not, consider including a grocery delivery service or a house cleaner on your wish list for must-have business services. If you can operate as a team and pitch in with your family members on weekends, you will save money. But consider the time and effort involved and choose your battles wisely. It may make sense to spend $100 to hire a house cleaner instead of spending five precious hours that you could otherwise bill out to a client at three times the amount. It depends on how busy you are and how much free time you have.

Setting Parameters

While everyone will be excited to hear of your new business venture, once the newness wears off, the reality of your project will set in. Friends who used to depend on you to go shopping with them or pick up their children after school may sadly realize that you just aren't as available as you used to be. It is best to head off disappointment by sharing your schedule and availability before feelings become hurt or misunderstandings happen. You might post a note at your front door that you are "in your office working" in case visitors drop in and interrupt phone conversations. However, although you will be happy to have your new business take up your energy and your focus, you should remember to balance your life and take time for yourself as well. Consider setting aside an afternoon or evening so you can catch up with buddies. Spending downtime with family and friends can even end up making you more productive.

If you are serious about taking the leap to become a wedding planner, consider starting slowly. Keep your existing job, or consider going part-time until you build up a good client base and resources for referrals. It will make your life hectic, but will help keep you financially sound and less stressed in the long run. You will know when the time is right to focus only on your wedding business. It depends on your financial responsibilities and how quickly your business takes off.

Support Systems

Peer and networking groups, social clubs, and volunteering can all help your business life as well as your personal life. I still belong to a book group that I joined when I first moved into my town fifteen years ago. A few years ago, one of my book group friends called me to enlist my help for her sister's wedding. At first blush, she just wanted "a little help." The final event involved two tents, limos, two bands, and loads of other vendors to support their at-home wedding. You will be your own best salesperson, so don't be afraid to share your passion with the world.

Frequently Asked Questions

1. *Is it really necessary to have a sitter when I work? My child is only six months old and sleeps most of the time.*
   If you are serious about your business, you should approach it as you would any other job. You wouldn't take your child to your office if you worked for a large corporation, so why should you expect to have one ear on the monitor and one on the phone with a client? Noise from children or pets and other distractions in your home will make it harder for you to portray yourself as a true professional. If you can't bear to bring your little one to a day-care center, consider an in-home helper who can attend to his or her needs immediately. It will take the pressure off you when you are in "work" mode and help set the stage of professionalism for your clients and family.

2. *I have so much work to do; do I really need to take a night off to play? Plus, I love my job!*

Yes! Take a break! You deserve to refresh your spirit and body, and it will allow you to come back with new ideas and a fresh approach to each wedding. If you love the business so much, consider a visit to a flower show (you will be getting ideas about the latest blooms and arrangement options), museum (creative ideas on which to base future wedding themes), or to the gym to work out (you will look and feel great when you visit your clients). Even the Bible suggests a day of rest, so take it whenever you can.

3. *How should I schedule my workday? Is it necessary to work from nine to five?*

By all means, fit in that exercise class or trip to the dentist when you can. That is the beauty of having your own business. A flexible schedule is one of the best perks, and you will more than make up for it when you work fourteen-hour days on the weekends during a busy wedding season!

4. *Should I give up my weekly tennis match or book group meeting with my friends because of my new company?*

Not at all. Incorporate your lifestyle into your new business. Maybe you want to pick and choose the outings that mean the most to you, or make the most sense with your new work schedule. If weekends will be busy and balancing all your extracurricular activities more challenging, focus on the activities that will help maximize your time. Consider attending an exercise class with a group of pals, or play golf with both a client and a buddy to meet both your personal and work goals.

Developing Your Business

Once your heart has helped you make the decision to begin your company, you must use your head to start off on the right foot. Consider the name of your company. Will you fly solo on this new venture, or team up with a trusted friend or associate to form a partnership? What other professional resources will you need to put all the business matters in place? Will you need to take out a loan to purchase the first few items to get your office running smoothly and professionally? These are the questions you should ask yourself to ensure a solid foundation for your business.

Setting Up Your Company

Start gathering information about your options on the Internet, your local library, or in small business magazines or books. Although there are basic steps you will take, there are many different options available to get the right fit for you and your new business. Seek advice from other local planners or people you admire who have the size and structure to their business that you aspire to attain. Whether your goal is to have several assistants, multiple weddings each month, a separate division for destination weddings, stationery products or wedding accessories, study the paths taken by the planners you wish to emulate. Ask to look at their business plans and quiz them on their achievements and mistakes to help you avoid errors from the start.

Your local library can be a great and inexpensive resource. Government agencies like the U.S. Small Business Administration will have basic guidelines and tips to get you started. You may even have a local office in your area, or you can visit online at www.sba.gov. Local professional groups or the chamber of commerce can also be a great resource for helpful tips and guides. Professional organizations like the Association of Bridal Consultants (ABC) or

International Special Events Society (ISES) will have monthly chapter meetings that may cover business topics. By attending these events or visiting their Web sites, you may also find members with whom you can network or obtain advice.

Don't be afraid to ask how they got started. Take a look at their business plan or one from someone in another small business. It is also a good idea to ask advice from retired business owners. They have weathered many a storm over the course of their careers and may have valuable words of wisdom to share. Contact your local office of the Service Corps of Retired Executives (SCORE) for more information or for members who would like to offer guidance. You may find a mentor who can walk you through the setup and important policies for successful small business management.

Your Business Structure

Where do you start? First, consider your business structure. Are you the kind of person who likes to work solo, or do you work best when you can brainstorm or create your wedding visions with an officemate? Do you feel you could use the help of another person to balance your skill set and round out the offerings you will have for your clients? While sharing the burden and excitement of your growing business with a professional associate may appear to take the pressure off of you at the start, it will also bind you legally to another individual in most aspects of your business. There are several other choices, and your selection will affect how you are taxed and the type of recordkeeping you must do. From sole proprietor to corporation, there are differences and unique requirements for each choice. Let's take a look at the basic components of each, as well as the pros and cons.

Sole Proprietor

This is the most common and simplest form of business ownership. One person owns all of the assets and liabilities. The owner has exclusive control of the business but also total financial responsibility to the full extent of the assets of the business, as well as the owner's personal assets. It is relatively simple to complete the necessary documents once a name search is done. If the name of the business is not the same as the name of the owner, a Doing Business As (DBA) certificate must be filed in the city or town hall where the business is conducted.

Pros:
Exclusive control of company; simple process.

Cons:

Personal liability for all financial obligations to the extent of all personal assets.

General Partnerships

Starting a partnership would mean finding a kindred spirit who shares your drive and passion for the wedding business. It should also be someone you work well with, who balances your business style, and who is willing to approach the business in a serious manner. You and your partner will be sharing in the profits as well as the losses of the business, according to your respective ownership interests. Partners owe each other the duty of utmost good faith and loyalty. The relationship is governed by a written agreement, but if they do not have one, it is governed by statutory provisions. DBA certificates must also be filed and a separate tax identification number obtained from the IRS.

A limited liability partnership is the same as a general partnership, except that some of the state statutes permit partners to limit any liability caused by the partner's negligence or breach of contract to their investment in the partnership. In any case, a partner is still liable to the full extent of their personal assets for their own liabilities incurred.

A limited partnership is when the general partner has full liability and management of the business and the limited partners have limited management. Their liability is limited to their investment in the business.

Pros:

Partners can divide up the work, such as sales, administration, and site visits. They can cover each other during vacations and illness. They can work together and take on larger and more complicated projects. While the partnership must file a tax return, it pays no income taxes, as the profits and losses flow from the partnership return to the partners' individual tax returns.

Cons:

Liability is still an issue. Each partner is personally liable for any obligation incurred by another partner. Thus, a partner is responsible to the full extent of that partner's personal assets for any liability incurred by another partner, through contract or negligently causing someone injury, whether or not that partner has anything to do with it or even has any knowledge of it. Partners may find that they do not get along, and it can be difficult to carry on the business. Partners need to clearly define their roles and anticipate what will happen to the business in the event that one partner ceases to work due to disability, death, or otherwise.

Incorporating

By incorporating your business, you form a legal entity solely for the purpose of conducting business. A person or group of persons form the business entity and elects a board of directors to control the company. This board in turn can elect officers to run the business on a daily basis. Many are closely held corporations, which means the shareholders are also the board of directors and officers. It becomes the business, apart from the individuals who run it. Ordinarily, a corporation bears a separate burden for taxes and liabilities.

Pros:

The main benefit of incorporating is the avoidance of personal liability. If there should be a lawsuit, the corporation would be held responsible, not the individual.

Cons:

Recordkeeping becomes more detailed, and the fees for running a corporation are higher. Articles of Organization must be filed with and approved by a state government, as well as annual reports with attendant filing fees. Bylaws must be adopted and followed along with minutes of meetings. These filing formalities must be adhered to, or a creditor could impose liabilities for the corporation against the shareholders as if there were no corporation. By filing a Subchapter S election with the IRS, you can avoid the double taxation and pass through income and losses of the company to your individual tax returns.

Limited Liability Company (LLC)

This is also a separate business entity created by the provisions of special state laws. It is like a corporation that has made a Sub S election to be taxed as if it were a sole proprietorship or partnership, except that it doesn't have some of the limitations that Sub S corporations have, such as restrictions on the different classes of stock, number of owners and management, and tax arrangements.

Pros:

Profits and losses are noted on individual returns, but the LLC is held liable for any liability issues.

Cons:

More recordkeeping than a sole proprietor or partnership, similar to a corporation.

Once you have you laid out the foundation, take a look at what you will build on it. The best way to start is to put it in writing. As a wedding planner, you know the importance of details, so start the business planning process the same way by paying attention to every detail. How will you describe the wedding planning services you will provide? Will you break out your services to include full or partial packages, or a la carte shopping for brides? Why would clients select you over someone else? When you start to identify the purpose of your company and how you will achieve your goals, you can work off of this outline to chart your successes and make the necessary changes along the way to ensure you reach your goals.

Research

Put in the time before you go after your first client to make sure you start off on the right foot. Here are some tips to save you time, money, and stress.

Uncover Opportunities

I once was doing some online research and realized a very exclusive community in my area did not have any wedding planners listed in the chamber directory or on Google searches. I decided to pay a visit to venues and restaurants that would host weddings or have the opportunity to use a planner with their clients. I presented a postcard with a beautiful photograph on the front and a snapshot of my services and how I could help make a wedding day stress-free. Within a week, I got a call from a prospect and booked my first destination wedding with one of the venues. It ended up being a fabulous multiday, multi-event destination wedding for a wonderful out-of-area bride. Keeo your eyes open for opportunites for new businesses.

Identify Competition

Check your local wedding or social directories or Yellow Pages for wedding planners in your area. Try to find local directories, specialty magazines, or newsletters to check on advertisers in the area of weddings. Research online for planners and study how they market their businesses. What can you offer that is different? How can you put a spin on your company to generate more interest or create a niche market? Identify whom you are up against and prepare yourself to go into battle well informed.

Identify Industry Growth Potential

Read up on wedding trends and changes due to economic or social conditions. When you present your services, you must make sure you do so in an appropriate way. Weddings in the 1990s were lavish and over the top. Because economic conditions were strong, purses were fairly open to provide the ultimate for the wedding experience for the guests. In the early 2000s, the focus changed as wallets tightened. While weddings tend to be somewhat recession-proof—they don't necessarily get canceled or postponed, just scaled back—they still may require some artful touches to create a dream wedding for the budgets you are presented with. If you can offer your clients suggestions on how to get the most for their wedding budget or create the look they want without breaking the bank, it will help get you business and a reputaton for providing valuable service.

Identify Potential Markets

As you scan the Web or read up on business opportunities, look for areas that are ripe for event services. Match this with your interests and skills. If your business pages or event directories show a slew of wedding venues, transportation companies, and florists but no planners, take note. If there is a nearby community that seems to be ripe for wedding planners because of socioeconomics or new event sites that are ideal for weddings, you may want to focus more of your attention in this area. Market segments could be based on geographic territories, types of services, types of customers, or even budget levels. Consider visiting the service providers that complement the wedding celebration, like limo companies, photographers, or florists, and ask if you might leave your card for those customers who are looking for a planner. It will be just as helpful for you to gather their information to complement the services you can provide as you begin to build your book of vendors.

Consider your menu of services. It may make sense to offer "day-of" packages or "contract negotiations and time-line planning" to bring in smaller pieces of business and keep your workday filled. Planning fifteen smaller weddings might bring in as much income and satisfaction as two large events.

Identify and Quantify Market Share

Perhaps you are most comfortable working within a fifty-mile radius of your home-based office and want to work at select churches and reception locations. You will quickly be able to determine who your competitors are. Now take an honest look at what business they are getting and what would be left for you. Is there something they are missing that you could provide? Are they handling all the country club events but none of the hotel events? Develop your checklist of potential clients and wedding locations, and start doing your homework. This will give you a better sense of your opportunities. Perhaps you can team up with a facility that has yet to hold private events and help it build a "wedding package" for smaller, more intimate affairs. Be creative! Remember—it takes time to develop business, so be consistent and persistent with your efforts to uncover new opportunities.

Identify Your Strengths and Weaknesses

As you begin your research, you will see where your strengths are. If you are coming from a corporate background, you may be comfortable dealing with your clients on a professional level. You may have to develop patience and slow down your expectations to give brides and their families a chance to work through the many decisions and emotions that come up during the planning process. Perhaps you are well versed in dealing with the emotions of the social client but need to build your planning skills, like creating and maintaining budgets, time lines, and planning schedules. Whatever your background, it is always important to be honest with what comes naturally to you and what you may need to work on to be the best you can be for your bridal client.

Identify Your Marketing Plan

Decide what kinds of clients you enjoy most and how you will keep them in your portfolio. Although this may sound simple, marketing to the right client can be the most difficult part of keeping your business alive. As a small business owner, you will wear many hats. Just as important as your wedding planning hat will be your business development and marketing hat. It's what will get your business off the ground and running. This will be covered in greater detail in Chapter 6.

First, develop a plan of attack: How will you kick-start your business? Start a database of contacts, and keep track of your initial calls and plan for follow-up. It takes effort to develop a relationship with a client or a source of clients, so be prepared to pay your dues. Drop a note in the mail periodically. Develop a personalized incentive item with your company name to remind them what you do. Tie it in with the type of event service you will be offering. Consider showcasing your business at a local bank, business meeting, or event facility. Ask if you can set up a display table presenting various wedding looks for customers to get a peek at what you do. Most rental companies will let you borrow place settings and linens, knowing that more business for you may mean more rental orders for them. Include a photo album of your work or a slide show on a laptop. Don't forget to put out business cards or include a drawing for a free consultation. Any way you can get information about your new company out to the right client is worth considering.

Creating Your Business Plan

You may think the most important characteristic of being a wedding planner is creativity and patience. While it is true you must have these traits to work magic with the wedding client, running your own company takes more business savvy than social style. Consider these critical first steps to building a strong foundation:

Selecting a Business Identity

Now that you have done your research and have thought about your plan of attack, it's time to put it in writing. In selecting your business name, be sure to settle on something unique. Your attorney can do a check locally and nationally for duplicate names. Also check Web addresses, as you will want to use your company name as your Web site address for optimal exposure and to make it easy for new clients to locate you.

When I selected my company name, I wanted my identity to be tied into my company name. I added the descriptor "event planning and management" as a subtitle. (I always use it in correspondence or when introducing myself and my company name.) As time went on, I felt the need to update it a bit and have created a shorter, more succinct version, while still keeping my identity intact. My full company name has been shortened to "jsmoran, special events" for postcards, email tags or on name tags. This covered my need to clearly identify who I am and what I do. Other possible choices for your company name might be to use the word "wedding" in your title or a descriptive word for the bride to identify with.

Writing the Plan

Your business plan will be a measurement tool to evaluate your success. This is a document that formalizes your dream of owning your own business. This plan probably won't be used to present to investors or even to show clients or colleagues, but it will give you a sense of direction and confidence to know that you have a plan in place and a way to reach your goals. As you move through the changes in your business, look at it from time to time, to see if you are aiming in the right direction. It will also highlight gaps you may have and what you must do to really succeed.

Mission statement

What is the purpose of your business? Create a short, concise statement that you can build your business on. This might include your values and offer keys to success. It will also allow you to stand out from the crowd and show how your services differ and excel compared to the competition.

Sample statement:

> JSMORAN, SPECIAL EVENT PLANNING & MANAGEMENT, is a full-service special-event company focusing on celebratory events worldwide. We position ourselves as a resource to individuals and families to create memorable experiences through the flawless execution of special events and weddings. We help create unique events through creative planning and professional execution.

Objectives

What is the objective of your business? Why will you offer these services? What will you provide to your clients to improve the quality of their life and add value to the wedding planning process? This information can be added to your Web site and your marketing materials, and can also be used to measure how you have satisfied your clients' needs.

Here are some of the objectives I have included in my business plan and marketing materials:

- To design, execute, and evaluate events that support and promote social celebrations and activities surrounding the festivities of marriage.
- To offer a complete package of services to complement the wedding experience, including print, media, transportation, decor, and entertainment services.
- To offer a valuable service to the bride-to-be, fiancé, and any other stakeholders involved in the event by offering professional advice and suggestions that will help streamline the process, save money, and create a dynamic and creative experience.

Invitations and printables

Favors

Wedding cake accessories—toppers / knife / custom cakes

Calligraphy

Table cards and holders

Ceremony accessories

Decor and design

Photography/videography

Entertainment—church/reception

Honeymoon travel

Parties—rehearsal dinner / luncheons / golf

Credentials/résumé

Why should you start this venture? This is where you must take an honest look at what you are bringing to the business. Just enjoying parties won't cut it. Optimally you would have a track record of experience in event planning, or, more specifically, wedding coordination. The best foundation for your business would be to have worked in the hospitality industry with events or in an event-related industry dealing with the planning process. If this is a new endeavor for you and you're coming from another industry, you will need to build on what you have in order to sell yourself as a wedding planner. Decide where the gaps in your training may be and set out to fill them. If you are offering top-notch service as a professional, you must be able to deliver it.

In reviewing your credentials section, list all the jobs or activities that have led you to your decision to start your own business. Also list your plan to build and enhance what you already have. List the courses or programs you will enroll in, any certifications you plan to get, and education conferences you will commit to attending. This will show you are motivated to be the best and will be aware of the most current trends and event services. Consider joining a bridal or event organization. As an active member in the industry, you will ensure that your customers receive "state-of-the-art" advice by using the most up-to-date products and themes.

Sample Biography Listing Credentials

Having been a social coordinator for a top five-star hotel, I have covered all aspects of coordinating weddings within a specific venue. I have worked with new clients to ensure their wedding reception runs smoothly and that all the details are in place to make their wedding-day dreams come true.

I have interfaced with food services to create menus, in-house audiovisual services to provide staging and sound, and have hired outside decor companies and florists to enhance the theme and style of the weddings I've planned. I have built a file of contacts for many wedding support services in the area, such as florists, musicians, and transportation companies. I have also outsourced personal services, including massage professionals, beauticians, and hair stylists to meet the needs of the bride and her wedding party as they prepare for the wedding day.

While I have been responsible for many of the planning procedures, I have not had direct selling responsibility or the opportunity to work in a variety of venues or with a variety of caterers. There are some services I am unfamiliar with, such as graphic designers, calligraphers, and tent companies.

I plan to enhance my expertise by attending an upcoming conference and specifically selecting courses that will round out my knowledge. As a member of my local ISES chapter and the ABC, I will seek out additional vendor support and get referrals on reliable services from my colleagues. I will also enroll in the study course to become a Certified Special Events Professional or a Professional Bridal Consultant and aim for certification within two years.

This biography shows a solid balance of basic knowledge backed by an understanding of what is necessary to complete the necessary training to be self-employed as an event professional. This self-examination, coupled with a team of solid business professionals, could start you on your way.

Organizational chart

How will you manage your business? You will decide what layers and levels of support you will build on in order to run your business smoothly and professionally. If you are the sole proprietor, you will be the CEO or president. You can identify your support team as the group of professionals that help you reach your business goals. These may not be employees of your company, but they will provide the professional support required to manage the many details of running a business.

In chapter 7, I offer suggestions on developing your team, including vendors and support staff. In most home-based wedding planning businesses, the organizational

A Typical Organizational Chart

CEO and President: Patty Planner, Professional Bridal Consultant (PBC)
Duties: Business management, sales, marketing

Accounting: Doug Detail, CPA
Duties: Financial management, including tax planning and bookkeeping support

Legal: Larry Lawyer, Esquire
Duties: Legal issues, including contracts

Information Technology: Carl Computer
Duties: Computer support, including virus protection, program, and technical issues

Assistant: Abigail Able
Duties: Supports CEO with information gathering, clerical support, and assistance with vendor relations

Support Staff: Various Vendors
Duties: Provide unique services for each wedding

chart is fairly streamlined, listing the owner, professional staff, and additional support for planning and services provided by trusted vendors. Check the sidebar for a typical organizational chart for a wedding planning company. The basic components to help support a healthy business are listed, along with other duties and tasks such as working with calligraphers, florists, or entertainment professionals, to be brought in as needed and treated as outside services.

Marketing plan

Here you will state how you will launch your business. This is the path from your heart to your customer. Nothing happens without a sale, so this is a crucial stepping-stone in getting your business up and running. After doing your research, you should decide on the marketing path you will take. Choose the market you want to focus on and go for it. You may include an array of strategies, including direct mailings, advertising, or cold-calling. Remember that this may change as the economic or local business conditions change. Be prepared to review and update as necessary.

Sample Marketing Plan

To reach out to customers, I will participate in a wedding expo to showcase my services. I will develop a tabletop exhibit that highlights my personal style, the unique and professional character of my business, and my commitment to excellent service.

I will also join at least two professional organizations, such as the International Special Events Society or the Association of Bridal Consultants, and offer to serve on a committee. This will give me recognition in the special events community and provide opportunities for business leads and professional growth.

I will direct my sales efforts to specific markets and create a strong campaign that clearly defines my skills and the benefits of using my services. This marketing campaign will include developing a Web site and a brochure which will be sent to vendors such as florists, rental companies, and photographers to enlist their support in recommending me to their clients. All direct-mail pieces will be followed up with a personal telephone contact and periodic checks to pursue opportunities.

Operations plan

In a broad way, this section will identify the many skills and resources you will be using to facilitate the execution of a wedding. Begin building the directory of vendors that will support your wedding services. This will also show your understanding of what is involved with the planning process and also serve to broaden your support base.

Your support team can include invitation designers, caterers, florists, rental companies, production and lighting companies, decor and prop houses, and general staffing support. By incorporating these vendors into your plan, you are building the foundation to carry out your creative vision.

Sample Operations Plan

As a full-service wedding planning company, the services of the company will include creative planning, design and execution, vendor management, and evaluation. Each client will have access to an operations team that will consist of a wedding coordinator and support staff who will interface directly with clients and oversee all aspects of the planning. Appropriate and unique vendors will be secured to supply all necessary components of the event, and professional staff will support all levels of the planning, including administrative, staffing, and professional services.

The team will be prepared to offer twenty-four-hour-a-day service when needed for weekend and evening events, and will be available via cell and/or pager to address all client and vendor needs. The day-to-day operations will be driven from office headquarters, with a master resource file listing pertinent vendor contact information. Time lines and production schedules will drive the execution of events and provide valuable benchmarks for monitoring success.

Financial plan

While visions of financial success can be a driving force behind your new business venture, there are prudent steps you should take along the way to achieve financial freedom. Before you think about cashing your first big check from your first client, consider what you will need to do to get to that point. What funds will you need to start your company? How will you pay for your office supplies and marketing materials? How will you cover your operational costs? Most service-based businesses do not require a great deal of start-up funding. The items that you need may be purchased with savings, on credit, or postponed until your sales allow for such expenses. Here is a list of financial tools you should use to start and maintain your business:

Balance sheet

The balance sheet will give you a snapshot of where you stand financially at any given moment in your business. It compares the assets and liabilities of your business and is a measure of business worth. As a small business owner, you may not refer to this on a daily basis, but should you decide to apply for financing, it will give the bank or lender useful information. It is also usually included in the end-of-year reports that you will compile for tax purposes.

Income statement

Your income statement will be the benchmark of the health of your company. A primary goal in business is to make, not lose, money. Although there may be start-up costs in the beginning, your ultimate goal should be to realize a profit from the work you do. You may decide to donate time in exchange for promotion, such as sponsoring a portion of an event to be listed in a program directory given to all attendees at an event. This is a great way to get exposure, but be careful to choose your events and causes wisely, and balance your donated time with paid projects.

On a monthly, quarterly, and yearly basis, you should prepare income statements on your business. Many software programs will allow you to get updates at a moment's notice. Even if you delegate this task to a bookkeeper, you should know how to retrieve this information and monitor its accuracy carefully.

Cash-flow analysis

A cash-flow statement is a useful tool in observing how money flows in and out each month. Weddings can be seasonal and bring in income only during a specific time period. It's important to market your services wisely to try to spread out your clients throughout the year if possible. Unfortunately, expenses may occur on a routine basis (i.e., telephone, vehicle, advertising, and office supplies). By being aware of the flow of cash, you can plan accordingly to manage your business operations soundly.

You can also make observations on how to approach your business mix to allow for a more even flow of money. Perhaps you target holiday weddings to complement your summer brides. As a wedding planner, during the slower, off-season times, you could enhance your services by offering holiday stationery, in-home decorating, or party assistance.

Short-Term Goals

I operate most efficiently when I make up daily and weekly schedules and work off of a goal sheet. When you start your business planning, you will compose a short-term game plan. What are the goals you are setting your sights on for this month, and even this year? Break those down to the weekly tasks that will allow you to achieve them. If a short-term goal is to secure a bride for a wedding within three months, then back into how you can accomplish this.

First, you must send the message out. Use whatever methods you deem appropriate to share this goal with the world. Whether you tell family and friends, contact vendors you know, call on wedding facilities, or take an advertisement out in the paper . . . plan to take the first step to allow you to realize this goal. Getting new business might be one short-term goal. Getting your office set up might be another. Keeping your vendor list fresh, gathering new wedding resources and ideas, or preparing an article for a newspaper could be added to the list. Back in to how you can realize these goals by creating a time line and set your sights on achieving your goals.

Timeline for Reaching Short-Term Goal: Wedding Client Booked
Week One

- Contact ten associates and ask for a referral.
- Drop a note to friends and family, saying hello and sharing your dream with them.
- Make appointments with five wedding facilities to tour their properties in exchange for sharing your service presentation.
- Take an ad out in a wedding guide.
- Write an article for your local newspaper on "Ten Steps to a Stress-Free Wedding Day."
- Drop business cards off at bridal shops, caterers' offices, florists, etc.

Week Two

- Follow up with sales efforts.
- Create new contact lists if no positive responses are received.
- If you have received some responses, make appointments with those brides.
- Attend bridal fairs for ideas and leads.
- Exhibit at local bridal fairs.
- Contact wedding venues to showcase at any open houses.

Week Three

- Follow up with sales efforts.
- Make appointments with brides.
- Send and sign contracts.
- Start planning.

Week Four

- Continue responding to inquiries from advertisements.
- Follow up with venues and vendors.
- Follow up with potential brides.
- Continue planning events under contract.

Weeks Five through Eight

- Same as above—call, contact, and follow up.
- Respond to all inquiries.
- Make appointments with potential clients.
- Keep the planning process going.
- Hire help as your wedding business begins to boom!

Weeks Nine through Twelve

- Continue to incorporate prospecting for business into your weekly goals.
- Continue to manage new appointments.
- Continue the planning process with already-booked business.

Long-Term Goals

Your long-term goals are an extension of your short-term goals. By achieving goals on a monthly basis, you can look at what you are accomplishing over time. Long-term goals tend to be more general and broader in scope. They are less specific and task-oriented and more result-oriented. By breaking down the long-term goals into smaller components, you begin to see how you will achieve the results you are looking for with the many activities that will get you where you want to go.

Your long-term goals are the vision that keeps you going through the ups and downs of your business. As the entrepreneur, you will deliver this vision to your clients, vendors, and staff as you offer your services.

Here are some examples of long-term goals:

- To create a business that in ten years you may be able to sell, if you so desire.
- To plan twenty-five weddings (both local and destination) within a five-year period.
- To become a leader in an international special events organization.
- To become recognized as one of the top five wedding planners in your city.
- To develop a strong social-event planning company, planning two events per month.
- To grow your business to five employees.
- To become certified in the wedding or special events industry within five years.

To reach these goals, you can use your short-term time line to break each dream into weekly steps. The may include education, volunteerism, and investment of time

What It Costs: Professional Fees

Attorney: $150 to $300 per hour

Accountant: $500 to $2,000 consulting/tax returns

Bookkeeper: $25 to $50 per hour

Graphic Designer: $25 to $125 per hour, $500 to $1,500 per project

Web Designer: $25 to $150 per hour, $200 to $2,500 per site

and money. These goals will be achieved by the work you do on a daily basis to build your business and reputation. These long-term goals will be the vision of your company, so it is important to start thinking of these from the beginning. Be prepared to change them as your situation changes. The economy, wedding trends, and your lifestyle may create a dynamic environment for your business, but if you don't set goals, you will never reach them.

Frequently Asked Questions

1. *Should I hire a professional accountant or attorney to help get my business documents in order? I only have one client and it seems like an unnecessary expense.*

   I would recommend running any legal document or financial consideration by a professional before you get into a situation that may cost you more money than any initial investment in a professional would. The money you spend to develop a sound contract will help secure a professional stature with your clients, who will respect the fact that you've thought of all the details that may come into play during the planning process. Setting up a system to track your income and expenses can be daunting, and a few sessions with an accountant or bookkeeper can help you avoid costly and unnecessary mistakes.

2. *Do I need to have professional business cards printed, or can I do it myself on my home computer?*

   While many home printers are equipped for color printing and can take heavier paper stock, you need to consider the final product and quantity to decide whether or not it will be worthwhile to pay a designer to develop your marketing materials and a printer to produce them, or if it makes more sense to do it yourself. If you will need only a few business cards to begin with and really want some time to consider if your initial ideas for your company image are the best, then print a few on your home printer and see how they look. Professional printing can be costly, and you often need to order a large quantity in order to get the best value. Once you have polled your family and friends and really feel good about your materials, go for the highest quality you can afford.

3. *Which is better in the wedding market—specialization or generalization?*
    While weddings in and of themselves are a specialization of the event industry, within this discipline are many subgroups. Niches such as destination and multicultural weddings, same-sex marriages, and the like are all very unique subgroups that can provide you with the opportunity to set yourself apart from other planners. If you have knowledge of one of these unique areas, consider being the best and selling this as your specialty. You may even decide to write an article for a local paper or magazine to gain attention as a specialist in a certain area. You can still pick up other side events along the way, but it will allow you to draw attention to yourself as an expert in the wedding industry.

4. *Do I really need a Web site to promote my business?*
    I think you do yourself a disservice if you do not have a Web site. While the wedding industry is a high-touch and personal field, much of the planning is done online. Brides, grooms, and their families are used to getting information electronically, and being able to search the Web for services and products is commonplace with all ages and backgrounds. If you don't yet have a lot of photos or details about your experience, keep it simple with basic facts, and focus on your qualities and desire to meet their planning needs. You can use stock photos available for purchase online to enhance your written materials. A Web designer, while pricier than doing it yourself, can help make you look like a pro right from the start.

Dollars and Sense

While writing a business plan is often the first important step toward formalizing your dream of being a professional wedding planner, you will also need to put your money where your mouth is. The financial success of your business will be determined by how prudently you manage your money and your clients. Training and experience will be the best way to back up your service promise, but you must round out your talent with proper pricing and wise spending habits in order to achieve business success.

Determine how you can launch your business and stay financially sound right from the start. Will you be leaving other full-time employment to start your business, or will you keep your day job and fit in events on weekends or evenings? How will you manage your income and expenses and track your projects? In any case, from your very first project you should approach the process in a professional and businesslike way. This will help you during the planning stages, at billing time, and more important, as you evaluate the profitability of your business.

Planning for Success

There are many tools you can use to manage your company's financial success. You will need the right information to make the best choices. From spending money on supplies to charging fees for your service, the ebb and flow of funds in your bank account will determine the financial success of your new company. Remember, you are in business to make money. While you may have to invest some money at the start, your goal should be to come out at the end of each project or year with a positive cash flow. This means more money coming into your business than going out—money that you will proudly take as the profits of your business. (See the sidebar for financial terms you should be familiar with.)

Financial Terms You Should Know

Revenue	Money you take into your company for your services or products.
Expense	Any cost you incur in the process of doing business.
Budget	An estimate of all the costs associated with your business or project (expenses) and money you plan to bring in (revenue).
Cash Flow	A snapshot of your available cash at any given time to cover expenses due.
Profit	Your company's revenue less expenses.
Net Income	A company's profit after expenses and cost of doing business is taking into consideration.
Deposit	A partial payment made when purchasing services or products.
Fixed Cost	The cost that does not change regardless of your company's activity.
Variable Cost	A cost for an item that fluctuates with units of participation.
Professional Fees	Money paid to you for your knowledge, labor, advice, and creativity.

Wise spending during the start-up phase of your business includes investing money in professional services, education, basic office equipment, and marketing materials. This will give you the requisite foundation of knowledge to charge a fair wage in return for delivering excellent service. Without sufficient knowledge of your craft, it will be challenging to back up your service promise and earn the income you have budgeted for. Without a phone, basic computer equipment, or marketing kit (business card, presentation piece, and Web site), it will be difficult to secure your first client. (Check out the chart in the Start-Up Costs sidebar for an overview of what you can expect to spend from the start.)

Developing and Using a Budget

For both your business and your clients, a budget is essential to measure the flow of money. While a program like Excel can be used to track client budgets, your company budget is best developed in a professional program such as QuickBooks by Intuit or another similar accounting suite. This will allow you to review your income and expenses with the click of a mouse. With the right program, you can invoice clients, pay bills, issue checks, and track the financial health of your company. I often supplement this with my own spreadsheet for goal setting and more detailed descriptions.

For every wedding, the budget will assist you in managing both your time and the creative advice you offer your client. The following budget comprises a client's available or allotted funds, the project scope, number of attendees, and breadth of services. I will review specific budget components in more detail later in this chapter, but it's a good idea to start with an understanding of the basic elements of a wedding budget.

Shannon and Donald's Wedding Budget

Category	Items	Amount
Print:	save-the-date, invitation, thank-you notes, napkins, matchboxes, postage	$1,200
Calligrapher:	table cards, signage, escort cards	$800
Ceremony:	church (or other venue) fees, altar servers, organist, musicians	$1,500
Reception:	site fee, tenting, production, lighting, permits	$5,000
Catering:	food and beverages	$10,000
Florals:	church, wedding party, reception	$1,400
Decor:	church, reception	$2,000
Transportation:		$900
Photography:		$2,500
Videographer		$2,000
Entertainment:	DJ, ensemble, other entertainment	$2,000
Rentals:	linens, china, tables, chairs	$3,500
Extras:	cake knife/server, cake topper, confetti at church, favors, name-card stock, signage, guestbook, wreaths, votives	$1,800
Operational costs:	postage, shipping, permits, licenses, sitting or tasting fees, labor	$2,200
Planning fees:	20 percent of contracted items	$7,360
Estimated total wedding budget		$44,160

When creating your budget, I feel that it is necessary to clearly outline an allowance for planning fees. When you agree to perform the planning services, you must commit to carrying out the project to fruition with the necessary components you have presented or the client has requested. You should estimate the time it will take to manage this process from start to finish and bill accordingly. Whether you charge an hourly rate, a percentage of services contracted, or a flat fee, negotiate a price that you feel will be worth your time and effort. Hourly rates can start at $25 per hour and go to over $100 depending on your location and the wedding market in your area. Your hourly rate will be based on your experience and the level of strategic work you will do for your client. If you will be researching products and locations, negotiating with vendors on pricing or developing high level design and creative treatments, you may want to charge on the high end of a pricing scale. If you will be following up on plans that the couple have already made and or handling day of coordination only, a flat fee may be a better pricing fit.

The Cash-Flow Statement

A cash-flow statement will let you take a snapshot of the financial health of your company at any given moment. As you track your projects and payment schedules, you may find periods of time where money doesn't flow in as quickly as you would like. Unfortunately, monthly bills (i.e., telephone, rent, utilities, and the like) will continue to be drawing from your bank account. If you develop a sound cash-flow statement, you will be able to examine the high and low periods of your business and begin to tuck your income away when it comes in to be ready for the draw on your account each month during the off times. With the sometimes-seasonal nature of the wedding industry, it's important to plan ahead in order to maintain a healthy relationship with your bank and your clients.

Take a look at the Cash-Flow Projections provided here to get an idea of the types of expenses you will have to prepare for, as well as possible income scenarios. You will notice that there are some months where monthly expenses will be higher than your revenue. It's best to have an account with money waiting to pay those bills as they arrive, whether or not you have a wedding that month. If you have a great December filled with lots of invitations or parties, tuck that revenue away for a month that isn't as busy. When you accept your first check from a client, especially if it includes money for items you will purchase on their behalf, you must spend and save wisely. Don't race out and buy that new phone or video software for your computer. Tuck aside what will be needed for credit card bills that will arrive in a month and use that credit card to purchase the wedding guestbook or runner that you need for your client. If you have helpers assisting you with wedding day setup or teardown, make sure you set aside enough cash to pay them at the end of the event. This will keep your relationship with your vendors strong so they will be there when you need them.

For your own cash-flow statement, consider what you will need to maintain a professional business and estimate these expenses at the start of the year. Will you be printing seasonal postcards to attract new clients? Will you attend a wedding expo to market your business? Would a class or conference be helpful in building your skill set? What are your basic living expenses? If you know that your expenses will be $30,000, reach for a portfolio of business that is double that amount to cover budgeted expenses and taxes. What's left over will be the profit from your successful business!

In terms of managing the finances of your growing business, be careful not to run out and spend all of your savings on office equipment or decor. You can certainly start slowly and use income to offset new purchases. Spend as you grow and keep your cash flow in check.

Pricing Your Services

Before you decide on your fee structure, research the competition. Find out what other planners are charging in your area. Is background and experience comparable to yours? Do they offer the same services? How much competition is out there for what you will focus on? Is there a real need for what you will offer your clients?

Set your pricing based on what the market will bear, your experience, and your complete understanding of the scope of the project. I will be honest and say there were times when I undercharged for my services, and times when I underestimated the time needed to plan a wedding. In doing so, I have inhibited the clients' understanding of the planning process and the value of using a professional. In the bidding process, you are sometimes left without options, or you negotiate beyond a reasonable limit. Experience and changing economies greatly affect how you respond to these challenges. While the opportunity to make money and support yourself with your own business should be one of the reasons you go into business in the first place, it can be one of the most stressful and dynamic parts of event planning as well.

Cash-Flow Projections

Income	Jan	Feb	Mar	April	May	June	July	August	Sept	Oct	Nov	Dec	Income
Wedding Coordination	$5,000	$5,000	$5,000	$5,000									$20,000
Day of Services	$1,500	$3,000	$1,500	$3,000	$1,500	$3,000	$1,500	$3,000	$1,500	$3,000			$10,000
Parties		$2,500					$2,500				$5,000	$5,000	$15,000
Products	$500	$500	$500	$500	$500	$500	$500	$500	$500	$500	$500	$500	$6,000
Total Income All Projects	**$2,000**	**$6,000**	**$2,000**	**$3,500**	**$2,000**	**$3,500**	**$4,500**	**$3,500**	**$2,000**	**$3,500**	**$5,500**	**$5,500**	**$51,000**
Expenses													
Professional Dues & Publications							$800						$800
Office Supplies	$50			$50			$50			$50		$50	$250
Vehicle	$600	$600	$600	$600	$600	$600	$600	$600	$600	$600	$600	$600	$7,200
Tax Payments				$2,500									$2,500
Insurance				$800									$800
Telephone	$120	$120	$120	$120	$120	$120	$120	$120	$120	$120	$120	$120	$1,440
Equipment	$50	$50	$50	$50	$50	$50	$50	$50	$50	$50	$50	$50	$600
Industry Conferences	$800							$800					$1,600
Travel	$1,000							$1,000					$2,000
Marketing Expenses	$200												$200
Printing	$200						$200						$400
Postage		$100						$100					$200
Shipping													
Entertainment	$50	$50	$50	$50	$50	$50	$50	$50	$50	$50	$50	$50	$600
Total by Month	$3,070	$920	$820	$4,170	$820	$820	$1,870	$2,720	$820	$870	$820	$870	$17,390
Cash-Flow Analysis	$(1,070)	$5,080	$1,180	$(670)	$1,180	$2,680	$2,630	$780	$1,180	$2,630	$4,680	$4,630	$33,610

Show Me the Money: Different Ways to Set Your Fee

Percentage

One way to estimate the cost of your services is to figure out your fee as a percentage of the total budget you are managing. I try to use 25 percent as a benchmark. This is not always how the final numbers flush out, but it is a starting point. The rationale for percentage-based pricing is that you are bringing your time and expertise to the table for each service you are asked to coordinate.

Negotiations sometimes come into play. If you perceive that there is a value in taking a certain project (whether to increase your own exposure or to gain contacts), you may want to make allowances in pricing. On the other hand, if you sense a client will need more than the typical amount of hand-holding, consider a fee-for-service or hourly rate pricing structure.

Fee for service

If during the proposal stages you get the impression that the project will require additional meetings, ongoing changes, updated progress reports, or the like, you may want to clearly define what you will do for the set project fee and offer the option of additional hours at an hourly rate. This rate would be based, as many professional industries are, on experience and qualifications. Project fees, depending on the simplicity or intricacy of the wedding, could range from $1,500 to $7,500. You should consider the planning details you would be responsible for, the size and location of the wedding, and the elements of the ceremony, reception, and associated events that you would be coordinating. When drafting your proposal, estimate how much time it will take for basic administrative duties, event management, promotion, and risk assessment and management. Break down each category into components covered and the estimated time it will take to carry out the tasks. This will give you a starting point for what you might charge for a planning fee.

Let's take a look at some scenarios. You are given a budget of $50,000 for a 200-guest wedding. If you get a sense that the event will be relatively easy to manage—for instance, it will be held at a local country club that you work with on a regular basis; the food service will be handled internally; there will be no rentals, transportation, or outside security or lighting needed; and the only additional services will be decor—you may be able to charge a flat fee that will cover roughly 30 hours of planning time. If you are currently charging $50 per hour, this would give you a fee of $1,500. Make sure you keep track of your time and let your client know if you are performing activities beyond the scope of the agreement. An addendum should be presented to cover the cost for any additional planning you may be doing.

In another instance, if the wedding will be held 100 miles away, will need tenting, full rentals of tables, chairs, linens, lighting, and power, and you have been asked to coordinate outside services such as entertainment, photography, video, and florals, you will want to estimate a much greater project fee. Consider travel time, telephone, and correspondence time for all vendors, and multiple updates for time lines and production schedules. In this instance, you may quote 130 or more hours for planning.

You may also figure in a range of planning expenses based on delegating some of the tasks, for which you would pay a variety of fees. You may know you can pay an assistant at $10 per hour to handle clerical tasks, favor assembly, and on-site setup, while a higher fee would be assigned for creative design and event management. By accounting for various fee levels, you will arrive at a final project cost to cover your time and labor.

Hourly

Using the same projection format, you may decide to present an hourly fee structure and tie each action item into a cost line. This gives the client a clear picture of what it takes to carry an event to fruition and allows you to be appropriately compensated for your time. You may have to negotiate on your time or make alterations based on budgets. It will be up to you, the professional, to educate your client as to the value of your services. If you are pricing your services out of their budget, you should eliminate items that could be performed by the client or by the venue staff and handle only the tasks that are integral to the event's success.

The range for hourly fees could be as low at $25 per hour or as high as $125 per hour, depending on the type of task and the consultative value you will bring to the table. Remember: You will be paying for your own benefits, social security, and taxes out of the revenue you receive, so don't underestimate your hourly rate.

Commissionable rates / add-ons

In some instances, I have seen proposals with no line item for planning fees. The planner is compensated by adding a "handling fee" or "finder's fee" to all the services that are provided at the wedding. If you will manage the rentals, florals, linens, etc., you may be eligible for a volume discount, which you could take as a commission. The client will not know what this amount is, but should realize this is being done if there is no indication you are being paid clearly printed on the estimate or invoice. In this case, you would handle all the billing, submitting the total invoice to the client if asked to, and reducing the amount paid to the vendor by the agreed-upon percentage.

I personally try to avoid this method. I feel it is important to show your value to the client with a line item on the invoice. I also pass discounts on to them, showing the savings that they will realize by enlisting my services and using my power of purchase. I think this is a much stronger argument and showcases the professionalism of the industry.

Negotiating with Clients and Vendors

Clients

Playing the pricing game can be tricky and requires give-and-take on the part of both planner and client. Negotiations sometimes, but not always, come into play when going from the proposal to the contract stage. Use your professional judgment when it comes to matching your fees to the client's expectations. It depends on how much you want the business, the difficulty you will have in executing the wedding, and a look at any marketing value the event might bring to you. You may elect to discount your price, but always put the total value of the event on your contract to give them a clear picture of a planner's worth. From that you may deduct a percentage or a flat amount to reach a mutually agreeable price.

Vendors

There are times when the cost of the event can be altered by negotiating with vendors for more attractive pricing. If you can foresee using a vendor for multiple events, a "quantity discount" may be negotiated. You would pass this on to each individual client to support the value of using a professional wedding planner and your ability to gain these discounts. Try to be sensitive to the suppliers' need to cover their costs. Some items that are fixed costs may be easier to discount, whereas other disposable or high-maintenance items may require a specific rate at each time of rental to cover any repair, cleaning, or labor costs associated with the item's use. Be cognizant of the delicate balance that is created with your vendors and respect their need to price their services in a professional way. When the budget allows, showcase their best products and compensate them justly. When the pencil is sharp, be creative on your selection of services to match your client's budget. Your valued vendors will understand the difficult task you have and appreciate you for using them for the variety of products or services they offer.

Keeping Track of Finances

Bank Accounts

It is imperative that you keep all of your business transactions separate from your personal accounts. You can do this by opening up a business checking account and using this for all business transactions. You should likewise have a business credit card to use for charging all business-related expenses. The neatest way to run your business is to keep a clear separation between business and personal expenditures. This will also help you at tax time and validate the operation of running a home-based business. You may also want to open up a few store or vendor accounts to begin to build credit relationship with suppliers. Pay for these bills using your business checking account to keep things organized and running professionally. Even when you want to withdraw funds from your business account, write a check to yourself and notate this as a draw to track your personal deductions from the business.

Budgeting

When putting together a budget for a wedding, you should take time to carefully estimate your costs in all areas. Step one is to start with the client's budget. You will need to fully understand the client's expectations for decor, cuisine, and entertainment, and counsel them on what can realistically be delivered. If their budget is $50,000, and the guest list is set at 500 people, you will be hard-pressed to offer filet mignon for an entree and get paid as a planner. Before you spend time working up a detailed outline of services, you must educate your clients. Offer options for a variety of food, entertainment, and decor that will fit within their budget and help them achieve their goal for the event. You may need to use your creative license and imagination to pare down certain areas to get the results the client is looking for. In the worst case, you may need to let a project go because there is no room for a planner's fee.

When creating a budget, I often have to present options and scenarios to help clients decide on the venue that is right for them. Here is where the value of using a planner comes into play. They appreciate your expert advice and the time you have taken to compile the list of options for their event. Once the research is done and the decision is made with a particular venue or selection of services, it's up to you as the planner to manage the project to stay within budget. For the example in the table that follows, the client was comparing the cost of hosting the reception inside a venue that would hold a maximum of 100 guests or to add a tent (with the associated costs for fees and decor) to include a total of 140 guests. To help them with their decision, I provided them with the facts and figures and then left it up to them to decide what their budget would allow. With the right figures in place, they would not be surprised by any unforeseen bills at the end of the wedding.

Cost Comparison between 100 Guests (with Reception Held Inside) and 140 Guests (with Use of a Tent)

Item	Quantity	Description	Price per	Total for 100	Quantity	Total for 140
Venue	100			$2,650	140	$4,900
Food	100	guests	100.00	$10,000	140	$14,000
Liquor: full service	100	buy own	$28.00	$2,800	140	$3,920
Service Only:	100	service only	$9.00	$140		
Transportation				$2,280		$2,280
Photography: 6 to 8 hours				$2,500		$2,500
Videography				$750		$750
Entertainment:						
DJ				$1,000		$1,000
Ensemble				$1,200		$1,200
Soloist				$100		$100
Church donation				$120		$120
Florals:						
Wedding party				$1,025		$1,025
Tables	10	tables	$85.00	$850	18	$1,530
Cocktail				$35.00	4	$140
Buffets/Other				$400		$400
Church				$700		$700
Room/Tent				$200		$200
Rentals:						
tables, linens, silverware, chairs (for 100) guests				$3,400	(for 140 guests)	$5,000
Tent						$5,230
Loggia				$1,400		$1,400
Invitations				$291		$291
Postage:	75	stamps	$0.55	$41	75	$51.30
Calligrapher:	75	sets	$4.50	$338	75	$427.50
Table cards	10	cards	$7.00	$126	18	$126
Guest cards	100	cards	$1.00	$100	140	$140

Item	Quantity	Description	Price per	Total for 100	Quantity	Total for 140
Extras:						
M&Ms				$414		$414
Butterfly release				$150		$150
Candy dishes				$40		$40
Miscellaneous decor				$200		$200
Knife				$35		$35
Guestbook				$25		$25
Wreath for limo				$13		$13
Shipping/FedEx				$20		$20
Total estimated cost				$33,343		$48,327.80
Planning fees				$3,500		$4,800
Decor Options:						
Draping tent & loggia	300	panels		$2,500		$2,500
Draping ceiling				$1,800		$1,800
TOTAL ESTIMATED COST				$41,143		$57,427

Tax and Financial Planning

The tax responsibilities and recordkeeping for a home-based business are drastically different than for an individual. A meeting with your accountant will help you to set up a system that you can stick with throughout the year and make tax preparations run that much smoother. Solid recordkeeping, controlling your expenses, and setting up clear lines between business and personal will lay a solid foundation for your home-based business.

Invoice (Based on Hourly Rate Pricing)

jsmoran, special event
planning & management
671 Main Street
Medfield, MA 02052
Phone: 508.359.7778
Fax: 508.359.7808
E-mail: events@jsmoran.com
Web Site: www.jsmoran.com
Invoice # 001
Date: 6/25/2008
Bill to: Betty Bride and Gregory Groom
123 Here We Go Lane
Happiness, IM 000000 USA

Project: Wedding
Terms: Due upon receipt
Consulting Services: Event Planning & Management: initial consultation, 1 planning
hour @ $125/hour = $125.00
Consulting Services: Event Planning & Management: 25 planning hours @ $125/
hour = $3,125.00
Consulting Services: Event Planning & Management, day of coordination, 10 plan-
ning hours @ $125/hour = $1,250.00
Total amount due: $4,500.00
It's been a pleasure working with you!

Invoice (Based on a Percentage of Wedding Costs)

jsmoran, special event
planning & management
671 Main Street
Medfield, MA 02052
Phone: 508.359.7778
Fax: 508.359.7808
E-mail: events@jsmoran.com
Web Site: www.jsmoran.com
Invoice # 002
Date: 6/25/2008
Bill to: Betty Bride and Gregory Groom
123 Here We Go Lane
Happiness, IM 000000 USA

Project: Wedding
Terms: Due upon receipt

Description of Services	Amount
Event Planning & Management: 25% of Estimated Expenses	$4,125.00
Event Planning Expenses: Venue	$2,000.00
Event Planning Expenses: Entertainment	$1,500.00
Event Planning Expenses: Caterer	$10,000.00
Event Planning Expenses: Decor	$1,000.00
Event Planning Expenses: Florals	$2,000.00
Total:	$20,625.00

Frequently Asked Questions:

1. *Should I start a business plan after I have acquired a few clients?*
   Why wait! The best way to turn your dream into reality is to visualize it and write down the details. Writing it down will help you to navigate the path to success by mapping out the resources you will need and the plans you will put into place to help you build your business. You may make changes along the way as opportunities arise, but at least you will have a goal to strive for and a plan in place to reach that goal.

2. *Is there any way to outsource help in writing up a business plan? Is that necessary?*
   There are plenty of resources available at your local library, the U.S. Small Business Administration (www.sba.gov), and at local colleges in their continuing education or night classes. You may even reach out to your local chamber of commerce or Service Corps of Retired Executives (SCORE, www.score.org) for a mentor to help you, or for general advice. While you can hire someone to do the work for you, or purchase a template online through a variety of sources (www.bplans.com, www.planware.org), going through the process yourself will help you to refine your skills as a professional business owner.

3. *How did you come up with your first-year budget?*
   The first-year budget should be set as modestly as possible. I used the equipment that I had, purchased only the items to brand and help me market my business, and added the extras as money came through the door. Don't go out and lease a fancy car or purchase the latest version of the iPhone. You are lucky to be in a business that does not require a lot of inventory; your biggest asset is your skill set. If you invest in anything, consider attending a course or conference to put you on the top of your game for your new clients.

4. *I am the only member of my team. Should I still write a business plan if I am the only one who will see it?*
   Absolutely! You may share this with folks in your networking group when you are chatting about your business growth, or with professionals that

help you manage your business, like accountants or attorneys. Having a business plan, even for a small company, helps you to think through the many responsibilities you have as a business owner and how you will plan for success.

Working on your first wedding may be what inspires you to launch your own business. Now comes the tough part: getting your second and third customers to turn your business dream into reality. Once you have your business plan in place and can visualize the path ahead, dig in with a well-thought-out marketing strategy. It will take a combination of creativity, style, planning, networking, and perseverance to get recognized as the go-to company for wedding planning services.

Assessing Who You Are

Be honest as you develop your written and spoken company statements. They should reflect your style and experience while showcasing the unique qualities of your wedding planning business. Your marketing materials should allow a potential client to quickly decide if you would be the best fit for their needs. From your company name to the way you describe the features and benefits of your company on your Web site or in your print materials, you are creating an image and company identity that will set you apart from the competition.

Take an honest look at who you are. What is your background? What are you most comfortable with in the planning process? What are your best assets? These would be the features you focus on in your marketing materials. Don't talk about destination weddings if you can't imagine working outside your own geographic area. Don't talk about production services if you are more comfortable with traditional wedding ceremonies and simple receptions. If a client surfaces who requires assistance outside of your comfort zone, you can always bring in a more experienced planner to co-plan with you until your confidence and skills grow. (I offered to assist a colleague as the "event planner" when the wedding she was planning grew to include fireworks, a faux skating rink, and live artists to perform at the reception—all of which would greatly enhance my own event-planning repertoire.)

What to Include in Your Marketing Materials

- Your branding or mission statement
- Benefits and features of your business
- Examples of events (with photos, if possible)
- Customer statements or references
- Awards or achievements
- Memberships in business or industry groups
- Leadership roles you hold
- Articles you have written
- Closing statement of why they should select you
- Your contact information

Developing Your Marketing Materials

Before you can print your business cards or consider the background colors for your Web site, you must first decide on what the style of your business will be, and how you will present yourself to potential paying customers. Developing a defining statement—one you can deliver quickly and confidently to describe your business—is a great first step. Another term for this is an "elevator speech." If you only had a short time to convince someone to hire you, what would you say? How would you share your passion for wedding planning with a potential client?

The next step is your company name. You will want to settle on something unique that clearly lets a potential customer know what you do with certainty; something that can stand the test of time. Consider your personal style, any specialties you will focus on, and the market you wish to attract.

Defining Statement

The first step to creating a successful marketing plan is to start with a business identity. Start with a defining sentence that brands your company in a unique way. You will use this as your marketing statement when you introduce yourself, meet potential clients, network at events, or visit vendors or venues. You can also refine this to use as your branding statement or "elevator speech" when you want to get your business message across clearly and succinctly.

Here are a few samples of possible defining statements.

Hi! My name is Claire of The Bride's Best Friend, and I specialize in weddings. I work with couples to make the details of their wedding flow smoothly, and I assist with the selection and management of the event vendors—florists, entertainment, linens, special transportation—to allow the bride and groom to create and enjoy memories of a lifetime! I can even arrange the pre-wedding fittings for the bridal party, help find gifts for attendants, and make travel arrangements for Aunt Sue and Uncle Phil.

Hi! My company, Weddings to Remember, creates weddings that incorporate unique and unusual themes and production elements. From butterflies to birds, from Maui to Madrid, we can handle enhancing your wedding ceremony and reception with unique props, backdrops, live entertainment, lighting, and decor, transforming your wedding day into a one-of-a-kind event. If you can dream it, we can do it!

Hello—my company, Weddings Away, partners with the bride and groom who are seeking a destination wedding experience. If you are a couple seeking a wedding adventure for yourself and your guests, I can help locate the destination of your dreams and coordinate all of the details to get hitched—without a hitch! From permits, licenses, travel arrangements, security, financial advice, and contracting, we take the stress out of coordinating your special destination wedding!

The Name Game

Your business name, logo, and business card will allow you to advertise in a formal way. This should support your defining statement and the goals and objectives that you have set up for your business. Once you decide on your company name, register it with your local or municipal government, or, more formally, with the secretary of state in your area. There are different types of registration that vary in levels of complexity and protection. A good attorney will walk you through the range of options and help you select the best method for you at this stage of the game. Your attorney will do a business-name check either locally or nationally to make sure it is not already being used by another business. Have a few company name options lined up, in case the name is already taken. When I started my business, I decided my own name would be my trademark. Luckily there were no other event planners who shared my name, so incorporating wasn't a problem. I immediately secured a Web address of the same title. My business had begun!

Your Company's Style

After you have selected your company name, consider how it will look in print, on the Web, or in other promotional items. Consider font style, colors of your artwork, paper stock, and whether you will design a logo. It is worth taking the time to consider your image and to create something you can live with year after year. The styling should fit your image and incorporate the key elements of your company. Whether you want a contemporary or classic look, carry your branding style throughout all of your marketing elements to create a professional and consistent image.

Print Materials

Although you may be enthusiastic about your business, unless you spread the word, it will be difficult to bring in customers. Networking and word of mouth can be an effective way to launch your company, but handing out a brochure or a list of references is typically expected once the initial introduction has been made. Having marketing materials ready to present to prospects and vendors is a must. You will want to include pertinent contact information (phone number, mailing address, and Web site address), as well as a brief summary of your company and what you specialize in. A list of references is also helpful to show you have a track record of satisfied customers. Testimonials—actual statements from past clients—will help folks decide if you are the right planner for them.

Getting Started

Your marketing materials will help customers decide if they want to hire you. If you have photos or descriptions of events that you have produced, use these as a foundation to describe your services. If you are starting from scratch and have done some

Tips for Marketing Materials

Font: Consider selecting a font that is available on basic Word document programs so you can always continue your style when sending proposals or follow-up documents. Even though you may want to select a script font that is elegant and romantic, don't use one that is hard to read. You want to strike a balance between creative elegance and something that is not confusing or overly fussy for the reader.

Paper: You may be drawn to colorful or elegant papers for invitations and cards, but they can be expensive if you want to produce marketing materials such as letterhead or folders for inserts and samples. Simple is often better. Check various sources for your paper stock to make sure you can get more than just one box and that the price is right.

Color: Using color can really jazz things up. For proposals and on your Web site, add photos of actual events you have produced to show potential clients firsthand your style in action. A good color printer will help you get your message across with pictures for those clients who can't visualize the work you do. You can also use color in your fonts to spice up your look; just don't overdo it!

Logo: A picture is worth a thousand words, and this can be the case when using a logo in your marketing plan. You will want to find a designer who will work with you to capture the flavor of your business graphically. You can use your logo on your business card, Web site, and any other printed materials you produce. Less is more, but don't be afraid to show your creative flair!

volunteer work, you may want to showcase your skills through a summary of these projects. If you were in charge of the decorating committee and managed a staff to develop a theme and create the event decor, this could serve as an initial building block. Photos or words of praise can be included to show the success of the event.

Be careful not to take credit for a project that you only had a small part in or were not directly involved with. If you helped another planner with an event, it would not be appropriate to describe that event in your portfolio or marketing material. If you feel you do not have enough to actually print a marketing piece, you should wait until you have done a few events on your own to create a personalized marketing piece.

I try to update my materials after every event by adding photos to my Web site and using new images in promotional materials. Consider printing a folder that has your basic contact and company information; then add inserts as you build your repertoire and client list. Make sure you are presenting yourself as professionally as you can. If your printer doesn't print photos nicely, have them done at a local photo shop.

In your materials, you should not only address the general elements covered in an event, but also reassure the client that you and your experienced support staff will be ready to deliver these elements as promised. This will show your clients that you understand the process and can help them work through the decisions necessary to create and execute a successful event.

Here are some sample marketing statements you can use on a printed postcard, in a newspaper or magazine advertisement, or on your Web site. You might continue with a bulleted list of specific tasks you can perform. Add photos, examples of work you have done, and testimonials from happy customers for a strong start to your marketing plan.

Weddings by Wendy

Make your wedding day memorable in every way! Enjoy the festivities while we handle the details. From the moment you say "I will" to the proposal to the memorable "I do" at the altar, let us help with the many details in between.

Weddings by Wendy offers wedding planning services with complete coordination of catering, linens, fine china and serviceware rental, small musical ensemble entertainment, and floral and theme decor to complete the look of your special event. When you have a dream, but no time to make it come true, let Weddings by Wendy come to the rescue!

Party Pizzazz

Just got engaged, planning your wedding, throwing a bridal shower or bachelor party? Whatever the festive occasion may be, let us help you celebrate with style! *Party Pizzazz* can assist with in-home parties or catered events at restaurants, hotels, or specialty venues, We complete the planning process with unique invitations, personalized decorations, full-service catering, beverage service, and entertainment to make your wedding or celebratory party the event of a lifetime!

Weddings Away

Have you always dreamed of a fairy-tale wedding on an exotic island? Do images of castles and bagpipes dance through your wedding dreams? Do you envision your wedding celebration as an adventure to be shared with your guests—but you don't quite know how to make it a reality?

Let *Weddings Away* come to the rescue, offering you ideas for an exotic destination wedding and guiding you through the many steps to make your wedding stress-free and memorable. From assistance on applying for the necessary documentation and information on country rules, exchange rates, and policies to help with group travel arrangements and wedding details, we create unique experiences for the bride and groom looking for the extraordinary wedding celebration.

Phase One	Phase Two	Phase Three
Select company name	Advertise in local or regional newspapers	Exhibit at a wedding expo
Develop mission statement	Include it in your brochure	Put it on your home page
Write your elevator speech	Practice it on friends or family	Use it at a networking meeting
Create print materials	Send to vendors, venues, prospects	Ask to have your materials on display at local venues or businesses
Design Web site	Track hits and maximize search engines	Update monthly with new info and photos
Join networking group	Go to meetings and follow up	Speak at a professional meeting

Becoming Web-Savvy

There was a time when an ad in the Yellow Pages was your ticket to getting business. Today's go-to resource for information is the Internet. Most prospects, even if you have come well recommended, will do some Internet research to find out more about you and your company. Today's couples will most certainly spend time online familiarizing themselves with customs, facilities, honeymoon spots, and personalized items and other wedding-related products and services during their personal planning process for their wedding day. Promoting your company through a Web site is a must. Check out chapter 11 for more details on getting your company online and using the Internet to build your business and help your clients with their wedding details.

Strutting Your Stuff

Selling tools can range from a simple postcard to a full multimedia presentation. Most wedding clients will not expect you to have a PowerPoint presentation to showcase your services, but they will be impressed by photos or video footage of weddings you have produced. It's best to show a full range of styles in your promotional materials. Given the varying tastes of brides and grooms, a sampling ranging from conservative to modern and anything in between is a good idea.

Try to show your organization, your creativity, and your ability to fit the needs of the client. If you can demonstrate that you took a bride's thematic idea to the extreme throughout the wedding process, prospects will be more apt to have confidence that you can do the same for them. Demonstrate your ability to react to last-minute changes or requests, and give examples of problem-solving skills that helped create a stress-free day for the wedding couple.

Promotional Tools of the Trade

Print: Use postcards, flyers, or pamphlets with text and photos to present your services in an impressive way. These are great to give to both clients and vendors to promote your company.

Portfolio: Create a scrapbook with photos and snippets of impressive invitations, programs, and guest favors. Use specialty paper or a distinctive album to show your style.

Web-walk: Give an online walk through your Web site with descriptions of photos and wedding stories.

CD: View a disc of photos from weddings and parties you have produced. Leave a copy behind for the client to view or share with family or friends.

DVD: Give a multimedia presentation that includes text, photos, and video clips of your most impressive accomplishments.

Developing a Marketing Plan

Getting the Word Out

Now that you have decided to formalize your wedding planning company, you need to go out and bring in some business. If you are lucky enough to have a few clients lined up, the pressure may be off for the time being. But one of the greatest challenges as a small business owner is to simultaneously market your services while handling current planning tasks. You should try to set aside a certain percentage of your time to focus on securing new business. Try to answer inquiries when they come in. Turn proposals around on a timely basis in an attempt to always have

future projects in the pipeline. In a perfect world, you would have another project
waiting for you immediately after completing one. Although this sounds good,
maintaining the perfect balance of business is seldom a reality.

Either you are too busy and can't handle the work coming your way, or you have
too much time on your hands between projects, wondering when the next event
will arrive. Both situations come with solutions. In the case of being too busy working on projects to market on an ongoing basis, develop a mailer that you can send
out monthly. Either write a newsletter or have someone do it for you. Perhaps a
student intern could create a monthly flyer that could be easily mailed to your target
list of clients. Take time to get your Web site up and running. It will serve as an ongoing advertising vehicle. Keep it up-to-date with new photos, client testimonials, and
event ideas. By staying in front of your existing clients and continually introducing
yourself to potential customers, you will keep the wheels of business turning. When
an opportunity comes up, you will be fresh in their minds.

Managing Leads

Developing a solid system for categorizing leads is critical in the first stages of growing a business. Some possible lead management tools (and there are many) run from
a basic Microsoft Office database, such as Access or Excel, to a more professional
management software system like ACT! by Symantec. Ask at your local computer

store for the latest and most popular software package, or do an Internet search to see what's new on the market. If you enjoy jotting things down on paper, you might want to develop a filing system using either file folders or index cards that contain key contact information and notes you make on an ongoing basis. After years of carrying a black book filled with business cards and addresses, I finally moved to an iPhone. I love being able to find everything in one place. While I still carry a notebook for jotting down ideas and daily lists, the important information gets logged into my Outlook program (either on my desktop or handheld), and is there for me to retrieve on my iPhone when needed.

Put together your target "sales" list and mark your calendar with a plan of attack. Most sales are made after making many contacts. It takes persistence and a belief in your services and what you can bring to this client to make a lead turn into a sale. The sources of leads can vary from word-of-mouth referrals, lists that you purchase, leads from newspapers, or research you do on a particular market you are targeting. However you develop your lead list, set up a system you can manage over time, and set aside a portion of your planning week to take care of the business of selling!

Advertising Options and Payback

Advertising can range from traditional methods such as print ads in local papers or directories to atypical methods such as speaking at a local chamber of commerce or writing an article in a specialty magazine. Typical methods involve creating an advertisement and paying a company, publication, or agency to run the ad for a specific amount of time. This includes Internet, print, radio, or television. If you target your audience and select a vehicle such as a wedding directory or a wedding program, it can help put your name on the map as an established business. I have found that general advertising does not target the audience you are looking for and can be costly. Types for advertising range from print (the least expensive) to television (the most expensive).

Trade Shows or Bridal Fairs

One way of getting in front of potential clients is by showcasing your company at an area bridal fair or wedding trade show. You will need to consider designing a booth and having plenty of print materials to distribute to potential clients. While this will require an investment of money and time, you will be reaching your target audience very effectively.

Specialty Associations

Involvement in industry groups allows you to not only continue your own training and skill improvement, but also gives you the opportunity to build vendor support and form bonds with colleagues that you can refer business to, or who could refer business back to you. A group of wedding planners in my area meet monthly for lunch to share vendor information, solutions to planning problems, and new wedding ideas or products they have discovered. They give each other the scoop on who is delivering the best or worst in vendor services. In a friendly way, these competitors work together to stay on top of their game.

Attending monthly meetings of industry organizations can put your face and business on the map. It takes perseverance and dedication to find an evening or two a month in your busy schedule to devote to marketing yourself and your services. When my children were small it was very difficult (if not impossible) to do. Between the travel obligations for my clients and my family's extracurricular commitments, it was impossible to attend a majority of these meetings. Over time, I made a commitment to become active in a leadership role in my local ISES (International Special Events Society, www.ises.com) chapter. By doing this, I have made business contacts and professional friendships that I couldn't live without!

There are several wedding associations that hold local and national meetings. ABC (Association of Bridal Consultants, www.bridalassn.com) and Association of Wedding Professionals (www.weddingpros.org) are two. Check the list in chapter 11, which includes both national and local resources. It can be time-consuming to attend meetings, but it's a great way to get to know colleagues that could refer business to you. People like to do business with friends, and networking events are a great way to get exposure and meet new contacts..

At the very least you should become an ISES or ABC member. Joining a professional trade group is an investment well worth making. The International Special Events Society is the premier organization offering education and networking within the broader special events industry, while the Association of Bridal Consultants will focus specifically on the wedding market. When you become a member, you have the option of joining a local chapter. Once you join, offer to sit on a committee, or better yet, begin to familiarize yourself enough with the chapter and offer to chair a committee. In any of the related hospitality organizations, the best way to reap benefits is to become active. Everyone will know who you are. And when someone is looking for a planner, your name will be the first on his or her minds.

Networking

Networking has become a useful marketing tool for selling your services in a more personalized, interactive way. It allows you to make an instant impression on a potential client and quickly assess the prospect. More personal than a mailer or flyer, a face-to-face contact allows you to get your message across quickly and effectively. It also allows you to ask the prospect to commit to a follow-up meeting, and, when possible, to set a date and time.

Networking can occur at professional meetings, social or civic gatherings, or with community groups. Check local papers for lunch-hour networking groups. Inquire as to the types of individuals or companies that are currently members. Assess the value of joining before spending any money on dues. If members could potentially use your services or refer business to you, it is worth at least trying out a meeting or two. Some groups have limits as to how many meetings you can attend before committing to membership. In any case, decide on how much time you have to give to this piece of your marketing strategy and choose the groups that best meet your needs.

Consider your target market and join a group that you think will afford the strongest leads. You will have to consider the referrals you will get. It may take a while for an actual lead to come your way, so be patient. The best way to approach networking is to go in with a plan. It's not a time to enjoy free food and wine; it's a time to gather leads, take notes, and make plans for follow-up. Check the Networking Dos & Don'ts sidebar for some pointers to get you off on the right foot.

Networking Do's & Don'ts

Do . . .

Arrive early.

Bring plenty of business cards and a pen.

Jot down information on each card about the person or when you will follow up.

Be ready; have a one- or two-sentence "elevator speech" description of what you do.

Gather more than you give.

Make a good impression.

Don't . . .

Try to juggle a plate of hors d'oeuvres and a drink while you try to shake a new acquaintance's hand.

Stick with people you know.

Spend more than three to five minutes with each person.

Oversell—plan to follow up with a full sales presentation at a later time.

List of Possible Networking Groups:

- Professional organizations
- Local visitors and convention bureau
- Chamber of commerce
- Vendor open houses

Hotels

Quite often, people will start the wedding planning process with the "place" they would like to hold the event. Hotel professionals may be able to offer their venue and catering services, but not the extended event services like entertainment, decor, invitations, lighting, or wedding favors. By coming up with a list of possible hotels that have the type of clients you would like to service, you may be bringing a service to the hotel as well as their client. By positioning yourself as a "preferred vendor" or "strategic partner," you add value to what the hotel can offer and expand your business through their incoming clients.

Places to Network

Networking opportunities can be found at industry meetings, at local visitors and convention bureau events, at chamber of commerce meetings, or even social gatherings. All of these offer an opportunity to tell your story and gather information.

Specialty venues

Specialty venues such as country clubs, ballrooms, meeting halls, museums, aquariums, or restaurants can offer the same opportunities as a hotel. Their clients will need all of the support services of a wedding professional, and by becoming a resource to the venue, you expand your own business opportunities.

Vendors

Vendors can be a major source of new business. Once you establish yourself with a group of professional colleagues, you expand your own sales force. A caterer may have a client who is looking for invitations; a tent rental company may be exclusive to a country club and be asked to refer a planner for a project. Vendors have become a major source of referrals for my business over the years. So treat your vendors well by thanking them for their quality work and products. In addition to sending business their way, hand write a note of thanks and include it when you attend an industry event; or invite them to join you for dinner.

Gaining Exposure for Yourself and Your Company

Volunteer

Donate a portion of your time—"What goes around, comes around." Stand out from the crowd . . . raise your hand . . . don't wait to be asked. Volunteer opportunities abound, from fund-raising events to industry or committee meetings. By sharing your time, energy, and creative ideas, you increase your visibility and make valuable connections in the community.

Educate yourself

Take courses on event-related subjects at a local college or university. Many schools are adding event-related courses to their continuing education programs. Most cities have seminars or conferences for the hospitality, meeting, and events industry. This is a great place to meet colleagues and pick up ideas. Whether the topics cover professional skill building, event design or trends, or give you business management skills, it all adds to the tools you need to grow and manage your business. Some courses, specifically provided by the International Special Events Society (ISES), can provide the basic foundation for achieving your Certified Special Events Professional (CSEP) designation. The Association of Bridal Consultants (ABC) offers the Professional Bridal Consultant designation (PBC). These, as well as other educational opportunities, add to your value, give you additional contacts, and let you have more to talk about when in a meeting with a client or following up with a prospect.

Be a leader

Share your expertise in your field, industry, community, or other industries. Each year I participate in career day at our local middle school by giving a presentation to the classes about my career and taking a group of students with me for "a day in the life of an event planner." Depending on the mix of students, we visit a site where an upcoming event will be held. Most recently, I scheduled a visit to a sport stadium in preparation for a company outing. In past years the field trip has included a visit to a design center for theme materials, lunch at a venue, and discussion with the chef regarding the menu for an upcoming wedding. I discuss theme and giveaway ideas with the students and even do some pre-event "shopping" when possible. These students not only get a behind-the-scenes view of a special venue, but they also get a glimpse of what goes on when an event is being planned. They also have parents who may need help with a particular celebration or wedding in the future.

Be seen . . .

Write articles for local and industry magazines, sharing your experiences. If there are publications that address event topics, perhaps you may offer insight on a venue you have used, discuss ideas about current themes or decor, or talk about challenges that your customers may face and offer solutions. Over the years, I have made contact with several event-related magazines and have had articles published. I let my colleagues know I like to write and they refer me on as well. The key for getting new business with this method is to get into magazines that cross over into other industries, and write on your specialty—weddings. When these magazines hit the hands of a bride who's ready to begin the planning process, you are the expert.

. . . and heard

Offer to speak at local or national events, within or outside your industry, at colleges, local schools, or public and charity events. This will help you define your skills and clarify your game plan.

Everything starts with a sale, so before the planning begins, get your client in place. Remember, somewhere out there, someone is looking for you and needs your services. You simply have to make the connection. If you have honed your skills and have an excellent service to offer, you will be able to respond to a client's needs. Believe in yourself and approach the task of marketing your service with determination and a positive attitude.

As you progress through the phases of getting your business up and running, be aware that you will constantly be defining and refining your skills. In your marketing materials, you will let customers know the changes that you are making to add value to their event experience. Take a long, hard look at your skills and what you do best and present them in the best light possible. Be visible in your industry, among your peers and competitors, and mostly, among potential clients. Consider all options; be willing to respond to changes in the business climate and with event trends. Take every opportunity to spread the word that you are an event planner who will make a difference.

Sample Marketing Costs

Booth at an expo: two-day show reaching 1,000 potential brides	$600 to $1,200
Custom envelopes	$74.99 for 500 envelopes
Custom return labels	$4.99 for a box of 150
Custom postcards	$19.99 for 100
Custom business cards	$3.99 for a box of 100
Custom memo pads	$7.99 a pad
Business cards	$119 for 500
Web site domain name	$4.99/month (after thirty-day free trial)
Advertising in a small-town single paper)	$50 a day ($20 to $40 for a paper
Sponsored search: Yahoo will place your ad at the top of the search page	$.50 each time someone clicks on the ad
Radio: ten-second spot in a metropolitan area	$250

Frequently Asked Questions

1. *Do I really need business cards and stationery?*
    To approach your business professionally, a business card is a must. You will be passing these out to prospects and leaving them at vendors' offices or venues that you will call on, ensuring that any and all potential clients and vendors will know exactly how to reach you. Don't clutter your card with unnecessary artwork or information. A logo, information on how to reach you (address, phone, fax, Web site, and e-mail) is really all you need. You may wish to add the logo of a professional group that you are a member of. Stationery will allow you to send proposals, letters, and thank-you cards and help create and keep your brand consistent.

2. *How expensive is advertising? Is there any free advertising that I can take advantage of?*
    Advertising can be costly and will require some thought before making any investment to ensure you are reaching the right audience. Other ways to get your name out to prospects include writing articles for local papers, speaking at meetings or community events, and donating your planning experience in exchange for a mention as a sponsor; all of these methods will give you solid visibility as a planner. Word of mouth and referrals can be a very effective marketing tool, so don't underestimate the cost of "tooting your own horn" to let people know about your wedding planning business.

3. *Does it make sense for me to pay to get on a preferred vendor list?*
    In some magazines you will have to purchase ad space to be listed on a preferred vendor list, but often you can simply request to be a featured planner with a vendor or rental company. This will depend on your relationship and how much work you do with them, and if they have had a chance to see you in action and know they can count on you to do a great job. Anyone who recommends you will want to be sure that you will meet their standards of excellence, so grow your reputation well and you will get extra mileage with your good name.

4. *Do I need a logo to make an impact with my company brand?*
   While a memorable logo can add style to your company's image, it's not a necessity. It can be costly to create and often will require special programs to open and reuse in other documents. If done properly, though, it can be a classy addition to your marketing materials.

All businesses are built upon layers of skills. While some entrepreneurs have a broad range of skills that help them deliver their business services on their own, most companies are made up of a palette of support personnel. Different staff members will provide administrative support, execute services, and take care of ancillary and customer service tasks. In the field of event planning, the owner of the business is typically the one with the creative and entrepreneurial spirit. However, to run a business successfully, you must balance the natural skills that you have with those you do not. Duties relating to financial planning, recordkeeping, and risk analysis need to be folded into your daily and monthly schedules. These functions are sometimes not the ones that are most easily accomplished or the ones that come naturally to the creative planner. Nonetheless, when you are starting a business, they are just as important as being able to take an event from start to finish. To succeed in your home-based business, take an honest look at your skill set and complement it with outside support when necessary.

What Skills Do You Need?

Running a successful wedding planning business takes a myriad of skills. Where are your strengths and where can you use help?

- Administrative skills: to manage recordkeeping, office organization, strategic planning
- Financial acumen: to develop budgets, maintain financial records, manage business finances
- Marketing savvy: to get new customers and maintain a steady flow of projects
- Interpersonal skills: to handle clients, staff, vendors, and prospects with professionalism and charm
- Creativity: to plan celebrations that are distinctive and unique and capture the style and dreams of your clients
- Logistical sense: to balance the many components of the wedding celebration (often under pressure!)
- Management skills: to juggle multiple projects, vendors, clients, venues (and do it all well!)

If you think you may need help in some of these areas, read on.

If you feel a bit overwhelmed by everything that's involved in your wedding business, don't fret. You're not alone. Everyone brings different skills to their business. The successful business owner will assess his or her weak points and hire or supplement as needed to build a strong business.

At the start, you may be able to handle many of the elements on your own. At some point you will realize it isn't humanly possible to design and produce the invitations, blow up all the balloons, create the centerpieces, be there for the rehearsal and the wedding day, and be home at night to do your billing and feed your pet pooch! Start by keeping a master list of tasks that must be done, and pick and choose what you will be able to handle yourself and what you will outsource. This will change depending on your project workload. Managing this balance will allow you to maximize both your time and the money you bring into your company.

What You Need to Know

Depending on your background, certain areas of running a successful wedding planning business may need some extra attention. What do you have for experience? While the process of planning may be very familiar to you, you may need to build your business management skills. Contact area planners or meet with facilities that use planners and see what they look for in hiring or relying on a professional wedding planner. If you feel like your skill set needs to be rounded out, become an apprentice or understudy with a full-service wedding planning company. Start with the lowest level possible to fully understand what goes into the overall process. Work through all the levels of activities from sales to setup. Attend industry meetings that offer educational topics. Read up on the latest trends. Take a class. Take all the necessary steps to lay a strong foundation on which you will build your company.

Back to School

When I decided to become certified as an events planning specialist, I signed up for a three-week course on fundraising to round out my understanding of what is involved in producing these types of events. I met some interesting people who also attended the class and learned new tricks on presenting budgets to the boards of directors of nonprofits. The mind-set for producing these events is very different from how corporate clients are handled, and it was an eye-opener for me. This was a class offered in my community through the Boston Learning Center, an adult education program that offers classes in many towns surrounding the city. It was not related to a degree program or university, but provided excellent insight delivered by a seasoned event professional. More and more degree programs are popping up, so investigate these options as well. I will cover more on educational programs for planners in chapter 11. Check your newspaper, high school flyers, or community college calendars for sessions related to the event or meeting industry. There may be more training right in your backyard than you thought!

Other skills that will be used in your start-up include business, management, sales, and technical skills. While you can certainly hire specialists to fulfill specific needs in these areas, when you are just beginning, you may not want to spend the money (or you may not have the funds available). Read a current book on time management, business planning, budgeting, and managing a staff. Many of these topics are covered in the best-seller list by authors boasting fresh ideas on the subject. Be willing and ready to change your approach so your business can get off to the right start.

The good news is that there are many professionals you can hire to help you when you need them, such as attorneys to develop contracts and accountants to help prepare tax returns. You should still have a basic understanding of your responsibilities as a business owner to maintain control of your business. Let's take a look at some basic areas that you will want to develop.

Business Skills

Running a business is no easy task. There are daily activities you must do to keep things running smoothly. First and foremost is the task of keeping track of your income and expenses. After all, one of the reasons you're going into business is to make money! Choosing a good software program like QuickBooks by Intuit will allow you to invoice your clients, write checks, keep track of account details, and help you in preparing for tax time. You can order personalized business checks through Intuit, which helps to present your company in a professional way. The program even allows you to personalize your invoices and track multiple jobs with one client. I found that the best way to become well versed in any new software program is to use it. Even a simple spreadsheet program like Microsoft Excel will allow you to keep track of itemized expenses and will help you price your events properly. Start using these business programs at the beginning and you will become very skilled at budgeting, forecasting, and controlling the finances of your company.

Management Skills

Managing the many personalities that you must deal with during the planning process can be one of the most rewarding—and frustrating—parts of being a wedding planner. In the world of event planning, you interface with the client, the setup crew, the chef, the servers, the photographer, the entertainer, and even the guests. You must be able to listen, assuage, persuade, consult, support, convince, and inspire—sometimes all in the same fifteen-minute period! It's a great idea to be aware of your own natural talents in this area and find ways to improve upon them. While it's easy to hire support on the technical side, or even on the selling side, you will still be the one who ultimately inspires, supervises, motivates, and manages your company and those who work for you. If you feel you are challenged in the "people skills" department, get some training. Take an honest look at how people respond to you when they are working for you. Watch how you deliver your requests. Do you show appreciation for work well done? Can you criticize constructively? Can you fire and hire people? Can you bring your creative energies and forces out in a positive and complete way, getting your point across and giving the event team the information they need to make it happen? All of these things are done in the course of running a wedding planning business.

I read business magazines like Fast Company along with design and wedding magazines for inspiration and fresh ideas. Even taking a course or a seminar can help strengthen your skills and keep your techniques contemporary and fresh. The local chamber of commerce or professional business groups will list these educational opportunities in the newspaper on an ongoing basis. The best way to stay on top of your management style is to ask for feedback and listen to the responses and take action. Be honest and critical of yourself and your events, and you will always be working toward improving what you have.

Selling Skills

As a company owner you are the best advertisement for your business. Present yourself with confidence. Exemplify the quality and style your company offers. Gather great success stories to share. Sell your company to your colleagues, friends, business associates, and potential clients. As you grow and can afford to take on help in different areas, this may be an area you expand. If you don't enjoy contacting people, talking on the phone, and asking for business, you can certainly hire someone to do this for you. Be prepared to pay for the service either in commission (most motivating) or for a flat fee. You will need to monitor the success of your sales representative to ensure you are getting your money's worth.

The greatest challenge is trying to sell and produce at the same time in order to keep business in the pipeline and create a continuous flow of income. By creating this balance, it will give your company financial strength and viability as a full-service, full-time business. Much depends on the economy and the sometimes-seasonal nature of weddings. It can be challenging to fit sales into your weekly calendar, but it's an important goal to set!

Technical Skills

Can you operate your computer with relative ease? Can you work through creating and presenting a PowerPoint or multimedia presentation? Can you design a flow chart and seating chart for a wedding? Can you compile a spreadsheet with complete costs to create and track a budget? If not, start practicing! You may want to grab *Microsoft Office for Dummies* or take a refresher course on using the key elements of a basic office computer program. You will need to achieve some sort of mastery in order to present and track your events in a professional way. Most of it just takes time and constant practice. I have learned basic programs through hours of use, but when a real computer glitch hits, I call "The Computer Guy," an independent repair technician who comes to my home (usually on the same day) to get me up and running again. He suggests updates or new products that will enhance my system, and even orders and installs them. This is an area that I definitely need help in, and it has been invaluable to find the right person to come to my rescue.

These are some of the various skill sets that come into play in running a business. While you don't have to be outstanding at all of these, you should be prepared to call on any of them in a given day. As your business grows, you will hire professionals to focus on areas you are least comfortable or familiar with, but as the owner and leader, you set the style and tone of your business. You will need to handle employee or vendor disputes, financial issues, planning challenges, or technical and legal predicaments. So tune up and get ready to go!

Project Management

Another area that will need ongoing attention is project management. I am assuming that if you are reading this book, you have a general knowledge of the wedding planning process. Perhaps you have worked for a caterer, a bridal vendor, or have even planned your own or a friend's wedding. You may have found it to be both challenging and rewarding as it planted the seed in your "this could be a career for me" garden. Hopefully it was more rewarding than challenging, but if you feel you lack knowledge in a certain aspect of the planning process, take some steps to improve your chances for business success.

Formal training in the area of event planning has become increasingly available through local universities and colleges in their continuing education courses. Courses specifically in wedding planning can be found through associations and private groups that offer training and credentialing both online and at seminars offered at various locations.

So take some classes and begin to round out your skill set. Even if you only plan to focus on one specific area of wedding planning, it's critical to have an understanding of how the many planning pieces fit in. As you learn more about the event process, you will realize the ongoing time commitment that it will take to run a project from start to finish. Even the smallest event requires the same elements. Each detail will need your undivided attention if it is to fit together with all the other details for a successful end result.

Enlisting Support

There are some areas of your wedding business that clearly require a professional eye. For example, services from an accountant, lawyer, or a computer expert will ultimately save you time and headaches when these areas are outsourced to a pro. Using professionals for these areas typically happens intermittently throughout the year, and can be included as part of your yearly company expenses.

To plan and execute your first event, you will need support. Besides the tangible items you purchase or gather together to design the event, your "people" tool kit needs equal attention. After you have taken stock in "how to," it's time to gather your "who to" list. You may have been clipping magazines and making sketches of wedding ideas for years, but a dynamic list of human resources is equally important to gather into a file.

The two areas that you will come to depend on for your wedding planning business are vendor support and staffing. Typically you will develop a list of names and specialties that will allow you to handle any request easily and professionally. Let's start with a look at possible vendors you will have in your tool kit.

Vendors

This list of possible vendors gives you an idea of the many resources you may need to access in order to cover many different tastes and styles. These professionals will have the latest and greatest tricks of their trade to make you truly shine as the wedding coordinator. There is no way I could keep up on all the most recent designs or techniques, and these experts help me to offer the latest and greatest to my clients. You may not need every type of vendor for each event, but it's worth starting to pull together your list; you can always add to it as you widen your circle of suppliers. By gathering the right team, your events can meet or exceed expectations time after time.

Vendor Resources

- balloon artist
- calligrapher
- caterer
- decor company
- DJ
- entertainment company
- florist
- invitation designer
- lighting company
- linen specialist
- makeup artist
- photographer
- power supplier
- rental company
- tent company
- transportation provider (limousines, buses, specialty cars)
- videographer
- wedding cake designer

Sourcing Out Your Staffing and Vendor Needs

Ask friends, colleagues, and business professionals if they know of people who would be reliable for the service you are looking for. Start gathering information and file it in an organized way for easy retrieval when you need it. I receive literature and brochures from suppliers and vendors which I file away until the right project calls for a certain specialized service or product. It's always best to get a reference or to ask a colleague if they have any impressions about a new vendor you are considering; this will help eliminate or reduce embarrassing or disastrous situations that often come from using an unreliable vendor.

Plan to maintain a thorough list of vendors to support a wide variety of wedding themes and ideas. You may not need a harpist, butterfly releaser, or videographer for your next wedding, but if the call comes in, you will have a reference number on hand.

Who are the best caterers—from elegant cuisine to casual fare? Where can you rent tents, chairs, linens? Where would you go for contract labor to help with setup and teardown? Where can you get balloons, and will they deliver? What do things

Vendor Criteria List

It's a good idea to have a checklist of what you are looking for in a vendor. Ask for a brochure, pricing guide, or link to a vendor's Web site so you can gather information beforehand to fill the needs of the many tastes and budgets of your clients. Plan a visit and inspect the quality yourself before booking. A vendor contract will also allow you to specify the details of their commitment to you and your client. See chapter 8 for a sample. Here are some items to consider:

- service specifics

- pricing

- quality of goods/services

- inventory selection

- references

- client list

- experience

- years in business

- service area

- staffing capabilities

- professionalism

- responsiveness to inquiries

cost in general? It's a good idea to have some budgetary estimates in place so you can talk knowledgably to your first clients. All of these "investigative" measures can be taken before you actually print your first business card.

Staffing Support

To complement your specialized vendors, you will need to consider what additional help you may need to get the job done: the crew you will need to set up or tear down your event; the people who will meticulously put together the giveaway bags or hand-tie the wedding invitations that you create. This "human tool kit" is the last layer of the preparation required to start your wedding planning business.

You may go into your business as the chief cook and bottle washer, but it won't be long before you realize you cannot go it alone. It may be difficult to assemble a team that will be ready and waiting to help with putting together invitations, dressing tables with linens, or parking cars, but these are the very real nuts and bolts of the event business. Where do you go to get support in delivering the quality you boast of in your marketing materials?

Staffing Support

Pre-Wedding:

- Invitation assembly
- Database management
- Ordering of favors or wedding incidentals, such as knife and cake server, votives, toasting glasses, guestbook

Wedding Day:

- Setup at ceremony
- Setup at reception
- Teardown

Post-Wedding:

- Packing and cleanup after the wedding
- returning rentals or borrowed items
- finalizing and delivering items to the bride or family
- following up with photographer, videographer

Students and Interns

Not a week goes by that I don't receive an e-mail from a college student looking for advice and experience. Due to the nature of the business, it is often feasible to use these young, ambitious event enthusiasts for weekend or evening events. It may be worthwhile to meet with them, do some preliminary screening, and compile a list to use for future projects.

Some schools have work-study programs that can provide paid or unpaid job experience. Contact the placement office at one in your vicinity to register for eligible students. I was fortunate enough to have two students interning recently, and they brought a fresh approach and unlimited energy to the many projects I had on my schedule. They were willing to work weekends and evenings and were computer-savvy, so they could research online for wedding supplies and favors. While it's time-consuming to organize the tasks you assign to them, it will ultimately save you time and let you move on to things that only you can do.

Working with Interns

The best way to use internship hours is to create a to-do list and itemize the specific activities that can easily be handled by a novice. While it takes time to create and update your to-do list, it's a great way to stay on track during the planning process, checking off the items as they are completed. Make sure you assign simple things that can be accomplished during the time the intern is in your office so nothing is left undone. If interns only work one day a week, it will be important to make sure they complete their tasks during that time frame. And always inspect what you expect, as you are ultimately responsible for the client's wedding-day success or disaster!

Relatives/Friends

Many start-up companies enlist family to support some of the activities in the early stages. I was lucky enough to work side by side with my dad in his moving and storage business from the time I was in high school. It offered me great training in business and served as the foundation for my event business. My family continues to help me with setup, teardown, video capture, and staffing whenever needed. My son, Kevin, is an amateur videographer and has made some excellent wedding and event videos. For some clients, his pricing is more in line with their budget, while still capturing the festivities of their wedding day. He also has captured set-up and behind-the-scenes footage that I have used in my marketing materials. Often my children have friends who are looking for extra work and are happy to staff coat check or serve as valet assistants. Just remember to formalize their involvement by compensating them and hold them to the same standard of professionalism, attire, and attitude as you do other employees. If you have doubts as to whether someone you are close to will work out, don't get him or her involved. Keep your company as professional as possible, choosing well-screened and well-trained workers to handle interactions with clients and important guests.

Colleagues

Once you begin announcing your new business, you will find many people who share your passion for the events industry. Keep in contact with them. They can be excellent referral sources for business you cannot handle, and they can also pass business on to you. You may be able to partner on a project that is beyond your scope at a given time, or use them to supplement certain areas of the event process. There's nothing better than having a staff that is used to the process and will approach the event in the same professional way you do. Don't forget to repay the favor by helping them out when they are pinched for staff.

Professional Organizations

The beauty of belonging to a professional organization like the International Special Events Society (ISES) or the Association of Bridal Consultants (ABC) is the unique network of professionals that can immediately become part of your team. Whether your weddings are in your local vicinity or are produced in locations around the world, a trusted team is ready and waiting for your call. Don't be afraid to perform a quick check of references to get an overview of the providers' full capabilities to best match your need with the appropriate vendor's skill set.

Trained Staffing Agency

Look for staffing agencies that can provide insured, bonded professionals to provide services such as wait staffing, food preparations, or bartending services. In my local area, Event Temps offers an array of trained professionals to help with anything from banquet wait staff to coat checks. It also offers full-service beverage catering for the planner looking to complement the wedding with both staffing and beverage service. It provides all drink-related products and brings out the latest in mixers, colored sugars, and the like. Make sure you choose a company that is fully licensed and TIPS certified, showing the completion of a certification program that includes all bonding procedures and training. TIPS certified bartenders safely serve guests and work to provide safe alcohol consumption, protecting both your client and your business. If you need trained event staff, such a company can support you with hard-working professional employees.

Setting-Up Policies

Information Gathering

For the most part, your vendor list should include vendors at various price points. Bonnie Katzman of BK Design offers unique interactive and specialty invitations. She is on the top of my list for innovative and impressive invitations. I know that when I use her, my client will be impressed with her one-of-a-kind wedding invitations. For budgets that don't allow for such a specialty approach, there are printing and mail-order companies for simple card-style invitations. It's important to do your research and be ready to assist customers with the right product or service for their celebration. If you can make a recommendation that fits their needs, you further solidify your value in the planning process.

Do your research well in advance to be ready for each client's requests. While you may be able to have catalogs and pricing sheets for some suppliers on hand, you may have to individually price out others based on the components the client is looking for. For instance, once you find a reliable rental or lighting company, you simply choose from their range of services—from simple to comprehensive—depending on your client's budget. In all cases, you should shop around for the best combination of dependability, quality of service and product, and competitive pricing. As the planner, you will be making the recommendation and pulling together your team of vendors. Selecting the best will only make your work easier and, ultimately, make you look better!

Job Requirements and Expectations

It's always a good idea to cover your performance expectations with each vendor. Things can change from job to job, and from client to client. A thorough review of your needs should be made in writing prior to each event. The production schedule you create will drive most of the timing, including arrival, set-up schedule, and picking up post-event. Your schedule will need to go even further, listing small details like who will set up the tables once they are delivered and who will put out the linens and collect them at the end of the event. All of these details should be confirmed prior to signing contracts and placing final orders. Remember, time is money, and if you will be paying your staff to perform duties that relate to vendor rentals, you should be compensated for it. You may have to include additional fees for this work, so consider these issues before you submit your final proposal to your client.

Evaluations

Just as important as thanking people for a job well done, you must also let them know when they do not meet your expectations. Sometimes, it can be caused by poor communications or unclear directions. Perhaps you did not stress the importance of lighting in the catering tent, or you did not share the fact that you needed handicapped access for guests. Even if you perform a pre-event walk-through, don't take for granted that a vendor will know what you want. Write it down. Include it in the contract. Discuss any special needs you may have well in advance of the actual event.

A critical discussion should happen with each vendor after the event to review what worked, what didn't, and what could be changed to improve the process for the next event you plan together. If done in a constructive way, this conversation will offer encouragement and demonstrate that you are interested enough in improving the relationship to create an even better event the next time around.

Lining It All Up

Once you have assembled the various support systems, you can begin to envision your company as an entity. You are the conductor of this fabulous orchestra that sometimes performs classical music, sometimes modern, and sometimes rock! As the conductor, you will be in charge of keeping all of the parts together and creating an end result that leaves your audience in awe. It is a sizable task, but with the right participants, it can be rewarding for everyone involved.

What It Costs

Education (Wedding Planning Certification Program—How to Start a Wedding Planning Business, 10-week class; QuickBooks, 2-day training: $1,300

Financial (QuickBooks Financial Software): $199 to $450

Event help or team members (interns, event setup and teardown, event workers): $10 to $20 per hour of service

Networking groups (one-year membership in the International Special Events Society or Association of Bridal Consultants): $185 to $450

Frequently Asked Questions

1. *Is it necessary to hire someone right away to help me? I only have a few weddings on my schedule, but one of them is tented and will be complicated.*

    A great way to supplement staffing for your weddings is to hire on a per-project or contract basis. You may agree to pay this person by the hour, day, or project. If you are feeling overwhelmed with last-minute details, consider inviting them to help out during the week of the wedding to handle pickups and drop-offs, or to be in one location setting up while you are with your client in another. You can't possibly be in two places at once—especially if you have a wedding that will be using two or more locations (ceremony site, photo location, reception venue), so bring in a helper. Don't forget to add extra labor charges in your proposal to offset any additional costs.

2. *I have contracted my first destination wedding. What's the best way to find the right vendors in another city?*

    One of my earliest events was hosted in New Orleans, 1,500 miles away from my home in Boston. The first planning step I took was to open my ISES (International Special Events Society) directory and call a fellow planner for a list of possible local vendors. Treat your destination wedding like a wedding in your own town by researching possible vendors and pulling together a list that you are confident can help you to create a successful event. Have backups in place, and get plenty of references to make sure you find reliable professionals in all areas. Word of mouth, referrals, and recommendations from local venues can help you pull together the right combination of services for a winning planning team.

3. *My pricing structure won't allow me to hire extra help. Where can I find good people to help me when I need it?*

   Try tapping into your local ABC or ISES chapter for student members or newbies looking for experience. Even event pros who are currently in between jobs might be interested in helping out, with the hopes that a vendor would recognize their talents and hire them full-time. Interns often will work for free and can sometimes bring friends who are willing to help with setup or teardown. Just make sure you establish clear expectations of attire and tasks to be accomplished, and that you fill them in on the nuances of the wedding in order to avoid embarrassing situations. A pre-event interview is also a great idea, so you can size up your potential staffer before the event begins.

4. *When will I know it's time for me to hire an employee?*

   Taking on the responsibility of an employee will require a commitment to having enough work and enough money to fulfill their expectations. If you can manage your projects with good contract labor, you may be able to avoid the extra overhead that an employee will bring. When you reach a point where you cannot service all the clients that are coming your way and cannot find the right people to handle your clients as you would, it may be time to bite the bullet and bring on an employee. Consider taking on an intern for a semester and see how he or she fares. If they catch on quickly, have a variety of good skills, and work hard for you, they may be able to transition into full-time. If you hit times that are slow, you can always have them focus on new business development until your client calendar is filled again.

While it's nice to think the process of planning a wedding will be a bed of roses, that's not always the case. It's not enough to have the latest design and decor ideas, or even to be able to work with the many vendors and clients you will meet; you must also take a hard look at the elements of each event that will open you up to liability and learn how to minimize your risk and increase the safety of your clients and their guests. While you should be aware of any changing regulations that affect the event industry, staying abreast of changing laws and requirements is best left to the professionals that work in the field of law risk management and insurance. For this reason, I suggest selecting an attorney who can guide you through the important task of creating basic contracts and updating these on a per-event basis as needed. Establishing a business relationship with an attorney is a prudent step to take for the safety and security of your business, as well as the events you produce and the guests that attend them.

Liability

According to attorney James N. Decoulos (Decoulos Law in Peabody, Massachusetts), who specializes in legal and insurance matters for event professionals, planners must be aware of liability throughout every phase of the event-planning process. Weddings are often emotionally charged and may contain elements of surprise that could result in disaster if not planned for appropriately. As you create dynamic environments with decor, offer catering services with food prepared offsite, select artists and entertainers that bring their own set of performance issues and dangers, you may become liable for damages sustained by vendors, venues, and event attendees. Some liabilities could include an injured guest, food poisoning, falling props, or misfired pyrotechnics. While most of these unplanned occurrences may not be the fault of the wedding planner, it is critical to show due diligence in taking all necessary precautions to avoid problems, including thoroughly researching the qualifications, experience, and reputation of everyone you deal with. Other potential issues involving liability include the consulting agreement contract, site selection, entertainment, subcontracts, security, and licensing.

Tips Regarding Event Liability

Attorney James N. Decoulos highlights the importance of addressing liability issues in order to avoid financial and personal disaster. Here are some tips from this legal specialist on how to respond to the tremendously complex issues surrounding event liability:

- Learn to understand what, in the course of conducting an event, represents exposure to liability and how best to minimize it.

- Embrace liability as your ally. Liability is at once a sword and a shield. Use the contract to both protect the planner and to bind the client.

- Don't overlook details about the fundamental business relationship between you and your client, especially at the proposal phase. This is particularly so for the last-minute booking that an event specialist accepts so as not to lose the business, with the added benefit of a chance to impress a client and gain repeat business. Even consideration to something as obvious as when and how the event specialist will get paid is cast aside as the parties focus their attention upon the components of the event so as to determine the price.

- A contract is not fully formed simply upon agreement of the price. In fact, the price is easier for a court to substitute than other necessary terms of a contract. Such contracts are referred to as "open price contracts." The price can be substituted from the marketplace, but there may be too many other details for a court to substitute, resulting in no binding relationship between the event specialist and client.

- Be succinct and specific. The event specialist must develop an ability to reduce to writing the essential details, both about what is being provided, and what is not. Does getting the state or city license mean paying for the licensing fee, or other costs, such as bonding or producing a floor plan? Oftentimes, a licensing authority will require special police and fire details at additional cost. When such requirements are discovered, and the additional expense becomes an adjustment of the contract price, immediate written notification must be made to, and an acknowledgment received from, the client.

- Short, simple letters written during the progress of work function well, even if only to document the efforts that are being made to fulfill the contract. Failure to do so will likely mean that additional expenses will have to be absorbed from profit. Failure to discover the state or city's licensing requirement in the first instance may subject the event specialist and the client to fines, or cease-and-desist orders, or both. You may be required to visit the local fire, health or building department to cover all your licensing requirements. It is unlikely that all such details will be available at the contract formation stage. Therefore, provisions should be made for modifications to the underlying contract in the course of performance.

- Carefully review the wedding specialist's client engagement letter. It should contain essential terms, such as the date of contract, date of performance, contract amount, deposit, progress and final payments, time and manner of payment, and specification of all goods and services to be provided, among other things unique to the wedding and related events. If a guarantee is offered, it should be worded to an objective standard. Use disclaimers to detail what is not guaranteed—for example, the weather and a good turnout.

Sample Consulting Agreement

- Duties (what you will be required to do for your wedding client)
- Payment (amount to be paid and when)
- Payment obligation and consequences
- Additional information (any other services or products you will supply, such as invitations or personalized items)
- Interpretation
- Cooperation
- Change Orders
- Important dates (date of wedding or related events)
- Delays and extensions
- Inspections and approvals
- Termination
- Abandonment
- Payment of fees and permits (any additional costs for the wedding)
- Deviations from laws and regulations
- Completion of event
- Indemnity agreement
- Applicable law
- Agreement to perform
- Signatures

Contracts

The safest and most responsible way to approach any business transaction is to clearly outline what you will do and for what price. Rather than approaching contracting as something that makes the wedding planning process more cumbersome, approach it as protection for your company and your client, and the formalization of your relationship that will add clarity to avoid any misunderstandings.

You may know as an experienced planner that you will perform certain duties during the wedding planning process, but your inexperienced client may not have a clue as to what is involved. It is your duty to outline the process so it is successful from start to finish. Take a look at the is a rough outline of a typical consulting agreement that I use. I would highly suggest that you consult with an attorney, preferably one who specializes in events management, who can draft a contract that contains the elements necessary to adhere to your state and city laws.

It's also a good idea to issue a contract to all the vendors involved in the wedding planning process. This will allow you to provide, in writing, basic facts around the celebration, and to state responsibilities of both parties. You can also detail special needs and requirements in this document. I've included a sample vendor agreement for you to review as well.

Duties

It is in this paragraph of the contract that you clearly identify the parties involved and the details of the day; then, list the specific category of service you will provide for them (the more details, the better). The categories might include event preplanning and preparation, production scheduling, vendor selection and management, theme development, budgeting, invitation design or coordination, production of gift item or favor, coordination of pre-wedding details, day-of coordination, support and staffing, and evaluation. You may break each of these down into sublists. For example, the "vendor selection and management" category might detail catering, rentals, linens, lighting, photography, florals, and transportation. You will go into more detail about vendors in your production schedule, time line, and vendor agreements, but it's a good idea to at least list the fact that services in this category will be researched and contracted with on behalf of your client.

Payment

Here you'll identify the payment agreed upon, along with the payment schedule. You might break this down into two or more payments based on the size and scope of the project. You would also list any expenses that you expect to be reimbursed for. These could include office or travel expenses that would be unique to the project. It would be appropriate to promise detailed lists of expenses and statement summaries to support the cost of the event as the event progresses. You should also identify your payment policy. This includes specifically when you expect advance payments and when they must be paid based on any bills you present.

Payment Obligation and Consequences

Just as you're committing to deliver a service, you are also asking that your clients commit to compensating you for your time. In this area you would identify

Sample Vendor Agreement

Parties involved _____

Name _____

Address _____

Contact information _____

Office phone _____

Office fax _____

Cell phone _____

Other phone _____

Wedding date _____

Location _____

Address / phone _____

Load-in time _____

Start time _____

Close time _____

Load-out time _____

Vendor services required _____

_____

Wedding planner services _____

_____

Breach of contract _____

Independent contractor definition _____

Payment schedule _____

Acceptance and signature _____

consequences of nonpayment that could include termination or cancellation of contract and collection or attorney involvement if necessary. Once again, this is not meant as a scare tactic, but as an admission of how seriously you take your relationship with the client and the obligation you are about to make.

Additional Information

This section of your contract acts as a request for cooperation from the client in submitting any information or materials that would be necessary or important in the planning and execution of the event. It does not spell out in detail all of the requests, but notifies the client that requests may be made for information, and that a timely response from your client to these requests must be made or the event cannot be properly scheduled—and you will not be responsible for this.

Interpretation

This paragraph acknowledges the creative license and interpretation that is integral in the event process. It states that the planner will be using their creative skills to develop the event, and once the theme or layout is approved by the client, the event will be developed accordingly.

Cooperation

Further outlining the dynamics of the event process, this section notes the need for cooperation by the client with the planner and any contracted vendors, and likewise commits to cooperation from the planner.

Change Orders

It's important to state the dynamics of the development of the event and the need to issue updates in a formal way. These "change orders" can be issued for signature during the course of planning without invalidating the original contract. Change orders may include additional items or expenses or updates to the scope of the event. They will also outline costs that would be associated with these changes.

Important Dates

The date section will formalize the start and end date of the project. It will also validate the time you will be putting into the planning. This section will complement your production schedule and time lines and show your commitment to the planning process. You can also reference expeditious and skillful proceedings and the use of sufficient labor, materials, equipment, and supplies to bring the event to fruition. Any reference to reports and schedules could be mentioned to further support the success of the event progress.

Delays and Extensions

Reference to delays due to the client or vendors or causes beyond the planner's control can be noted here. The communication of delays or of extensions and any necessary alterations in the schedule can be provided verbally and in writing. In most situations, a wedding date is set and the planner works from that time forward in allocating time to complete the planning process. It is not typical that a wedding would be rescheduled due to delays, but additional labor or time may need to be added if delays occur midway through. This could result in additional costs and would be submitted to the client through a change order.

In the event of delays due to the client, the planner would request an appropriate extension. This section could also include reference to any damages the planner incurs because of the delays, such as vendor penalties or deposits that may be forfeited. A mention of a time frame for settlement of any expenses and the use of arbitration can be made.

Inspections and Approvals

It's a good idea to show your willingness to have the client participate in any progress inspections during the course of planning. This not only shows your faith in your work, but also your commitment to giving the client what they want. If they should want to make alterations, it is best to do so before you are at a point where it would be costly or inappropriate to make changes. These inspections and approvals may be made during scheduled meetings, or more informally with spot checks of tabletop design, color, or material samples and schematic drawings, and should be documented.

Termination

This section is for the protection of your client should your client desire that you cease to perform your duties. Terms for payment to you for services rendered and/or a refund to your client of any funds paid for work not completed should be provided. The client is free to contract with another planner to reach completion of the project, bearing in mind that you are entitled to compensation for your work, your creativity, and the opportunities that you missed because you committed to this project.

Abandonment

Should the wedding be canceled by the client, this part of the contract will protect the planner up to the amount of time and expenses he or she has provided and incurred to date. This unfortunately can occur, and you will want to make sure you are covered for any deposits you have made, invitations ordered, or personalized products purchased that cannot be returned. Fortunately, I have collected partial payment from these clients, and try to end on a good note, in hopes that future opportunities for planning will arise.

Payment of Fees and Permits

As a planner, you may be required to take out permits or pay for fees on behalf of the client. This section acknowledges that these costs may arise. In some instances, the planner is required by law to file for permits, such as for tented events, events with pyrotechnics, or for events on public property where liquor is being served. It is the planner's responsibility to know what is required for each unique situation, but the client's duty to reimburse for these expenses. If you can budget for these in advance, you can avoid advancing expenses on behalf of the client and dipping into your own business checkbook.

Deviation from Laws and Regulations

You should notify the client in writing about any phases of the event that would deviate from laws or regulations before proceeding with the planning process.

Completion of Event

Here you will commit to removing any items at the close of the event, including equipment, rubbish, or props that were used in the production process.

Indemnity Agreement

You should request that should you incur injury, damage, or claim caused by the conduct of your client or your client's attendees to the event, your client will hold you harmless for any loss you sustain as a result.

Your client, based on their own or their counsel's interpretation and impression, may strike or modify this as well as any of the sections of your contract. I would recommend that in turn, you consult with your legal counsel and make any necessary modifications so you will continue to protect your business in the course of your relationship with the client. Depending on the reasonableness of the requested changes, you will probably work to modify the contract and move forward with the project.

Applicable Law

This short statement will define what state law will govern the contract, typically the state where your business is located or where the event takes place.

Agreement to Perform

The closing statement commits to perform the covenants stated in the contract. The signature lines, titles of all parties involved, and date follow this brief statement.

A contract like this will prove to be a useful and necessary tool for your business. The days when a "gentleman's handshake" was enough to formalize a relationship are, for better or worse, over. A formal written contract is today the best way to protect you and your clients. It also gives you and your business a professional and reliable aura that will protect both you and your many clients!

Permits and Licenses

The terms *permit* and *license* are interchangeable, and refer to any permission that must be issued by governmental authorities for any aspects of an event. When you contract to provide planning services, you will be expected to know what approvals are necessary to perform the event in a safe and legal manner, and you must make it clear whether you or your client will obtain the necessary approval. Never underestimate that a government authority could simply refuse to issue the approval, thereby canceling the event. You may find out that the approval will not be obtained only days before the event is scheduled to take place.

Such approvals are by local, state, or federal agencies in association with the use of pyrotechnics, tents, Dumpsters, utilities, the food service, parking and transportation issues, music use, or outdoor signage and banners. It is the responsibility of the wedding planner to know the situations that warrant prior approval and how to go about securing it. You must also consider the time it will take to obtain approval and plan accordingly. The associated cost(s) should also be considered and factored into the budget and your contract.

For example, a tented event where food and alcohol will be served and a fireworks display will close the wedding celebration will require an array of approvals. Begin with the clerk in the city or town hall where the event is being held for information on what boards or agencies will issue each approval. You may have to continue through to federal agencies depending on the situation. If you are not sure, ask. Discuss each situation with your vendors, venue staff, and fellow professionals. If they provide the service, such as the food or liquor, they may already have the approvals in place or might know where to apply for one.

In situations where music is being used or signage reflecting a copyrighted image is copied, as a planner you must know when the use is appropriate, legal, or ethical and when it is not. Fines and even lawsuits could result if you are ignorant in this area. To run your business as a true professional, take the time to research each situation and educate yourself regarding the proper use of copyrighted material. Your client will respect you for your knowledge and recommendations as you take the prudent precautions with your event design and execution.

Insurance

Despite all of your contractual and risk management precautions, your liability exposure cannot be completely eliminated. Make it a point to review with your insurance specialist what business coverage you should have. Let's take a look at the insurance policies you may have to consider. First, acknowledge that you are the key to the success of your business. Life insurance, health insurance, disability insurance, and key person insurance would all apply to you as the individual owning the business. You should also consider comprehensive general liability and property insurance at the very least, with options for other specialty policies such as cancellation insurance, employment practices, or business-interruption insurance. If you have employees, most states require that you provide workers compensation insurance, which you cannot avoid by calling someone you hire, yet control, a "subcontractor." You may also consider a policy for errors and omissions insurance to cover you for claims against your business for errors you may make in the course of rendering the professional service of event planning. These are but a few of the many options available to protect yourself and your company.

Locate a broker who comes well recommended, with experience in small business plans, home-based businesses, or, even better, with event or meeting management companies. A trusted advisor can walk you through the pros and cons, as well as the cost and feasibility of taking out each policy for you and your company. Ask your insurance advisor about the special risks you face, not only in your home-based business but also with the events you plan, and bring your coverage up-to-date to avoid legal or financial disaster.

Improving Your Risk Exposure

This overview of the legal and risk implications that you face as a planner may reveal areas in your own procedures that need revisiting. If you do not have a contract you feel is thorough enough, revisit it. Find a legal advisor who is knowledgeable about the unique features of special events, and seek advice on preparing your documents so you and your client are approaching your relationship in a professional manner.

Become more critical of the way you produce your events. Here are some important things to consider:

- Does the venue provide adequate food preparation and storage facilities?
- Will you require additional electricity to handle all production elements?
- Are the electrical wires or extension cords taped down so guests do not trip?
- Do you risk fire or explosion from the materials you use or the way you present them?
- Are any open flames well away from igniting loose fabric or decorations—and does the fabric you use meet local or state fire codes?
- Will your entertainment require any staging or rigging? Are all exits clearly marked?
- Is security in place for the safety of guests?
- Are all of your (or your vendors') permits in place to perform their duties according to the letter of the law?
- Are you using insured vendors?
- Are you named as an additional insured on their policy for the specific event

date you contract with them?

- Do you meet any state or federal regulations concerning the American Disability Act or other mandated laws for public events?

Once you have considered all of these elements, it's time to create a more formalized plan.

Creating a Risk Assessment Plan

Work through a risk assessment plan for each event. Examine the exposure to risk for each event and work to limit the occurrence of accident or injury. Here are some areas you should consider in your risk assessment:

- **Location**—consider access for cars or buses, guest entrances, tent placement
- **Guest profile**—young children, elderly, disabled, special dietary or religious requirements
- **Decor**—securing all decor items, including ceiling drapes, hanging items, stage decor, dance floors
- **Entertainment**—power supply, staging, and special equipment requirements
- **Transportation**—drop-off and pickup locations, rules regarding special services, such as champagne "toasts" offered by limo services
- **Cuisine and beverage service**—food storage, preparation, chilling and heating, guest allergies and safety
- **Lighting and specialty production services**—taping of any electrical cords, proper wattage, pyrotechnic safety
- **Safety and security**—special guests that require security detail
- **Evacuation procedures**—clearly marked exits, fire procedures

This is just an example of the kind of risk assessment plan you should be thinking about as you plan your wedding celebrations. I hope this section will reinforce the importance of your role as a planner, and how crucial it is to understand the risk you assume when you accept the responsibility of overseeing a wedding. If some of this seems overwhelming, I would suggest taking a course or completing an education session at an industry conference that deals specifically with risk and legal issues. Regulations and requirements are changing by the minute and vary from state to state, even from city to city. The most responsible and professional position to take is to be prepared. Know what your legal and contractual obligations are for the safe and smooth production of your events. Begin to pull your resources together and learn where you must go to create the event your client wants in a safe and successful manner.

Event Ethics

Ethical behavior in our society is continually under scrutiny. Whether you are a high-level official with the ability to touch the lives of thousands or a wedding planner who works with a few clients and vendors, you are responsible for your actions and how they affect others.

In 1987, a group of event professionals joined together and formed the International Professional Special Events Society under the direction of the founder, Dr. Joe Jeff Goldblatt, CSEP. Upon becoming a member of the International Special Events Society, participants agree to adhere to the ISES Principles of Professional Conduct and Ethics. Among other things, each member will "promote and encourage the highest level of ethics within the profession of the special events industry."

Acknowledging ethics as a component of your business policies can only enhance your reputation in the public eye. Still, ethics often involve moral considerations that can differ across cultures, geographic locations, circumstances, and professions. Unethical behavior could destroy business relationships, impact the finances of the parties involved, or leave an unprofessional mark on the industry in general. In other words, the questions and decisions you face in your business may not always be easy ones. Some of the ethical quandaries you will encounter include the following:

- Gift giving and receiving
- Taking credit for other people's creative ideas
- Failure to acknowledge others' contributions to your events
- Use of others' material in your promotional work

Payment Policies: Commissions or Kickbacks?

The event industry is continually seeking ways to create an increased professional stature. Training and accreditation along with a focus on ethical behavior contribute to the good reputation of an event professional in the community. This can be translated into the planner's ability to charge professional fees for services and the client's acknowledgment of how much value the planner brings to the event experience.

When considering your own standards, take a look at the mission statement you created in your business plan. What elements can you reflect on during the event-planning process? As you negotiate with vendors or clients, are you behaving in a manner that you are proud of? In the case of accepting gifts or compensation, is it a necessary part of giving or getting business? Does it affect your ability to make sound, unprejudiced decisions?

Creativity: Who Takes Credit?

We are in a highly creative field, and it's sometimes difficult to protect our unique ideas. We share them with clients and colleagues in the proposal process and during networking events. Nothing is worse than presenting a fabulous theme and ideas for execution to a client who then does not hire you and ends up doing the event on their own. As frustrating as it may seem, you must realize that ideas are not legally protected and do not in and of themselves make the event successful. Rather, it's the combination of all the components that take the event from a mere idea on paper to a successful reality. It's all in the risk assessment, the attention to detail, the wealth of information on sources for products and services, and the way you as a professional planner carry it all out to perfection. It's the training and attention to building your business that allows you to be the event creator, not merely a staff person who follows an instruction booklet.

There are no right or wrong answers to some ethical questions. It is up to each individual to make the choices they are proud of and that represent the behavior of a professional. If you have used a colleagues design idea for your event, ask their permission and acknowledge them when ever you can, whether it be to your client, your professional associates or on your website. If you worked with someone on an event and have a great photo, make sure you add the footnote of who designed and created the look. Honesty will help you build your reputation not only with clients but with your industry colleagues. Others will be more willing to lend a helping hand when asked, when they know they will get due credit.

What It Costs

Life insurance, health insurance, disability insurance: $800 per year and higher

Lawyer: $100 to $400 per hour

Contract-writing software (a feature of iDo wedding software): $299 to $399

Legal guides for small businesses: $3.99 to $61.99

Frequently Asked Questions

1. *I am covered under my husband's health insurance and I am the only member of my team. Do I even have to worry about insurance?*

   If you are covered under another plan, then you will not have to add the additional expense of medical or health insurance to your company's budget. But you should consider the other personal lines of coverage, such as life insurance or disability and business insurances (i.e., liability, or errors and omissions). It's best to consult with a professional insurance broker. If you can find one that has experience with small businesses, even better!

2. *How can I protect myself from business scams? What types of threats should I know about?*

   There are many Internet scams that may come your way having to do with loaning money or investing in a business or philanthropic venture. Any e-mails that have suspicious senders should immediately raise the red flag. Another prevalent scam that has recently affected wedding planners is an inquiry from an international client looking for wedding planning assistance. This e-mail will even contain a photo, and the "client" will offer to send a deposit in the form of a money order. They will request that you pay all the vendors and will forward you the money beforehand. Typically, they will have a short turnaround time and want to use vendors in other countries. My advice: If you don't know the client or can't meet with them to verify their authenticity, pass on the offer if it seems at all suspicious. This is also true for actual, legitimate clients who have big ideas but end up not having the budgets to support them. If some of your clients should want filet mignon but have only a hot dog budget, let them know what they can truly afford. If they are willing to make concessions, then it may be a match. If not, you may want to pass on signing a contract with them.

3. *How do I offer insurance to my team members?*

   If you are using contract labor, it may not be necessary to offer insurance. Once you enter into an employer/employee relationship, this changes. It's best to refer to your state or country's requirements and get the advice of an accountant or insurance professional.

4. *I have recommended a caterer to a wedding client. At our initial tasting, the caterer presented the pricing to the client, including all the costs of coordinating rentals and an on-site coordination fee. How can I avoid vendors trying to usurp me in front of a client?*

   It seems as though a caterer would cherish a planner's involvement and acknowledge the fact that a strong partnership will bring more business their way. It is shortsighted to think that it would benefit them in any way to take a planner out of the equation! Unfortunately, more vendors are trying to expand their services and this can sometimes cross the lines of ethical behavior. Make sure your vendors know your capabilities and their role when they work with you. Working with a professional planner can let the vendor focus on what they do best, whether it is food service, rentals, entertainment, or transportation. Most caterers I know would not be the best choice to help a bride with her invitations, seating chart, program booklet, travel arrangements, or floral selections. It sounds like some education needs to take place if this caterer wants to stay on your preferred vendor list!

Wedding Planning Basics

Running a professional business is no easy task, but if you set reliable systems in place that you follow from the initial inquiry to the parting good-byes, it can be a straightforward and rewarding venture. Not every prospect will turn into a client, and not every client will have the same needs. What all clients do want and deserve is professional advice and a successful wedding day. And you as a planner can play an important role in making sure everyone walks away with a smile.

Client Assessment

I like to begin my relationship with a prospect with a telephone call to gain an overview of what their expectations are. An initial conversation will allow me to uncover their style, budget, and basic facts about the wedding, as well as test their potential as a client. In a twenty-minute conversation, you should be able to tell if they are serious about using a planner, and if they can afford your services. Many times they may need planning assistance but have a budget that will not allow them that luxury. In these cases, I may give tips or suggestions for planners that are in their price range, or supply leads on services they can contract themselves. After this first meeting, even via telephone, you can gather the facts needed to really "wow" them at a face-to-face appointment.

Face-to-Face Meeting

Once you are able to assess their needs and resources, it's wise to schedule a face-to-face meeting. If you have decided to pursue a client relationship with this prospect, make an appointment to introduce yourself and your services and to create a powerful first impression. Meeting with the couple will allow you to begin a more personal relationship with them and gain a better understanding of their style and what they're looking for to create a wedding that truly suits them. This is when you will present an overview of your services and continue to gather information about your client. You should refrain from giving specifics on pricing; it's best to keep your conversation general until you have a better understanding of the wedding elements. If you know they will only want specific duties on the day of the wedding, you may be ready to present a contract for the day of services only, but save the more-detailed pricing until you have had a chance to review your meeting notes and draft an official proposal.

You should leave this meeting with a clear idea of their needs, style, and their response to any ideas you have presented to enhance their wedding experience so you will be ready to create a proposal of services. Ask about their time frame, their decision-making process, and how many other planners they will be interviewing. If you are one of twenty, you may treat the proposal process differently than if you were the only one they planned to interview. Leave your appointment knowing when they will want a response and when they will be selecting their planner. Set a meeting for your proposal presentation, and be sure to ask them what issues are most important in their decision-making process.

I use the following questionnaire as a starting point and reference sheet for my wedding clients. It includes basic details, but also additional information that helps me to understand their background and preferences so I can offer suggestions that will better fit their style.

Putting It in Writing

Even if you know your new client well, a contract is a great way to clarify expectations and formalize your agreement. I cover this in more detail in chapter 8, but be prepared to state the basics and update it if necessary. This contract will go into your wedding binder along with other documents that track the planning process. I also like to start my binder with a business-card sleeve or a sheet listing all the vendors and important phone numbers. It can be a time-saver when you start making follow-up calls and need to have easy access to those numbers.

Presentation of Proposal

While you will be excited to present your ideas to your prospective clients, one of the most important things you can do is to listen. From your first meeting to each one thereafter, listening is perhaps the one skill that will make your client engagement a success. Remember—you are not designing the wedding you think will be best for them, but the wedding they want. It's best to establish this at the outset so everyone will be prepared as they work through the many changes that will take place during the planning process.

Wedding Questionnaire: Details and Responses

Names of couple: _____

Wedding Date: _____

Bride's Name and Address: _____

Groom's Name and Address: _____

Wedding Location: _____

Wedding Party Size: _____

Wedding Party—# of attendants, family: _____

Bride: # of attendants, family: _____ Groom: _____

Guest List—Size: _____

Religious/Ceremony—Preference: _____

Other Contact Information—Parents of bride, groom, other invested parties:

_____

_____

Estimates and Descriptions

Catering—reception: _____ dinner: _____

beverages: _____

Florals—bouquets, arrangements: _____

_____

Decor—to include ceremony decor (arbors, runners, confetti, row ribbons/florals, draping) and reception decor (lighting for tents or room decor and lighting):

_____

_____

Linens—style, colors, overlays: _____

_____

Rentals—ceremony chairs, reception tables, chairs, buffets, serviceware:

_____

Entertainment—for ceremony (ensemble, soloists) and reception (band, DJ):

_____

_____

Transportation—limo, trolley, horse and buggy; to and from location: _____

_____

Photographer—any photos before, plus formal, engagement photos, wedding
photos: _____

_____

Videographer—on-site, DVD for presentation at wedding: _____

_____

Tent Company: _____

Hairstylist / spa / makeup: _____

Production Company—lighting, power: _____

Wedding Planner—at other locations (includes the planner fees, or if there are
contacts at the rehearsal dinner, and/or reception location, their information
may be included here): _____

Ceremony—cost of donation to church: _____

Rehearsal Dinner—location, # of guests who pay: _____

_____

Post-Wedding Brunch—location, # of guests who pay: _____

_____

Gentlemen's Activities—location, # of guests who pay: _____

Ladies' Activities—location, # of guests who pay: _____

_____

Destination Support Requested—transportation, accommodations, gift
baskets, special requests, and other needs: _____

_____

The Planning Process

Besides your proposal and contract, be prepared to present an honest outline of the schedule of events leading up to the event. As the pro, it's your job to map out a reasonable path to their wedding day and help them stay on track. Wedding clients will often want personalized items that take extra time to order, proof, approve, and arrive on time. Orders for items like save-the-date cards and invitations should be sent out on a timely basis, and you will keep them apprised of the deadlines. Don't forget to include payments and deposits on your schedule to keep the fiscal side of your business healthy as well.

Here is a brief outline of the types of items you will want your client to consider during the planning process:

Wedding Planning Time Line

Nine to Twelve Months Before

❐   Set an initial budget: _____

❐   Secure wedding date and time: _____

❐   Consider type of wedding (day/night, indoor/outdoor, formal, or casual): __

_____

❐   Research and select ceremony location: _____

❐   Select reception location: _____

❐   Select entertainment: church, reception: _____

❐   Select caterer if not already provided by the reception facility: _____

_____

❐   Select florist: _____

❐   Consider printed materials: save-the-date cards, invitations: _____

_____

❐   Confirm officiant at the ceremony: _____

❐   Set aside blocks of hotel/motel rooms for out-of-town guests: _____

_____

❒   Book photographer: _____

❒   Book videographer: _____

❒   Consider other entertainment: _____

❒   Send invoice for first payment: _____

Six to Nine Months Before

Select wedding cake vendor: _____

Consider rehearsal dinner or other events: _____

_____

Book transportation: _____

Order invitations: _____

Four to Six Months Before

Request guest list if you are sending out the invitations: _____

Select and order the invitations and stationery: _____

Select calligrapher if needed: _____

Confirm vendors: _____

Two to Four Months Before

Confirm the menu and catering details with the caterer: _____

Prepare all maps and directions for the ceremony and reception: _____

Order personalized items: cake cutter, topper, guestbook, etc.: _____

Set the dates and times with the officiant for the rehearsal: _____

Plan the bridesmaids' luncheon and any other parties: _____

_____

Design and print the program for ceremony: _____

Finalize the florist details, photographer, videographer, musicians, etc.: _____

_____

Arrange the necessary accommodations for out-of-town guests: _____

Plan a rehearsal dinner (time and place): _____

_____

Confirm the wedding cake details with the baker: _____

Send invoice for second payment: _____

Six to Eight Weeks Before

Mail invitations and announcements: _____

Coordinate portrait sitting with photographer for the newspaper: _____

_____

Hire the limousine or other form(s) of transportation for the wedding: _____

_____

Four to Six Weeks Before

Decide what the menu is going to be for the reception and estimate guest
count: _____

Confirm florist details and delivery times: _____

Plan the seating for the reception as well as other details for the ceremony and
reception:_____

Start writing placement cards or order calligrapher's services: _____

_____

Help choose the music for the ceremony, first dance, parent dances, and party,
and give information to band, DJ, or other musicians: _____

_____

Send invoice for third payment: _____

Two to Four Weeks Before

Continue checking on ordered items: _____

Confirm vendors: _____

Order permits or licensing where needed: _____

Send invoice for fourth payment: _____

One Week Before

Review any seating details: _____

Finalize the seating arrangements: _____

Review all the final details with planner re: vendors (photographer, videographer, musician, florals, etc.): _____

_____

Give a final head count to the caterer: _____

Confirm the availability of the musicians and vocalists: _____

Delegate responsibilities to reliable individuals on the wedding day: _____

_____

Finalize rehearsal dinner arrangements or other events: _____

_____

Send invoice for fifth payment: _____

_____

Organizing the Details

Even in the age of electronics, I still keep a binder (or two) for each client to hold all the necessary planning documents. Tabs separate the planning areas, allowing me to find information quickly when needed.

Getting Organized

Here are some ideas for your binder tabs to keep things at your fingertips:

Contracts

E-mails

Administration

Budget

Invitations

Ceremony

Cuisine

Rentals

Entertainment

Transportation

Decor

Extras: Items ordered

Planning Tools

Along with your supporting documents that will begin pouring in as you investigate options and place orders, you will also want to develop planning tools, including your planning time line and then the production schedule for the more specific wedding elements. Your production schedule, which will list arrival and departure times of your vendors and any special services they will need, will be developed from your vendor list and their contracts. Here's a worksheet with main contacts, key people, and possible vendors, along with the information you should gather to help manage the many services being provided.

Wedding and Vendor Details

Details: Payments due, arrival time, departure time, services they will provide, items to provide to vendor

	name	title	mailing address
Wedding party			
Groom			
Bride			
Groom's mother			
Groom's father			
Groom's sister(s)/ brother(s)			
Other			
Bride's mother			
Bride's father			
Bride's sister(s)/ brother(s)			
Other			
Couple's-family friends			
Vendors			
Photographer			
Videographer			
Florist			
Wedding cake bakery			
Transportation company			
Caterer			
Linens			
Rentals			
Rehearsal dinner			
Chef			
Site manager			
Restaurant manager			
Tent company			

	phone	cell	E-mail/Web site

	name	title	mailing address
Transportation company			
DJ/Musician(s)			
Wedding reception			
Conference manager			
Director of conferences			
Reservations			
Chef			
Catering manager			
DJ/Entertainment			
Production company			
Church			
Pastor			
Associate pastor			
Organist			
Church coordinator			
Soloist(s)			
Services			
Hair			
Makeup			
Spa			

	phone	cell	E-mail/Web site

I treat the time line as an overarching tool for keeping on track, and I use the production schedule to specify the vendor and supplier requirements for arrivals and duties. You will also include minute-by-minute details during the wedding celebration to keep everything flowing smoothly. Take a look at this wedding-day production schedule:

Wedding Day Production Schedule

Time	Activity	Location	Who	Notes
8:00 am	Floral, decor setup	Venue	Florist, Planner	Leave napkins, linens
12:00 pm	Set up at venue	Venue	Florist, Planner	
12:00 pm	Bride hair	Salon downtown		
1:30 pm	Bride makeup	Venue	Makeup artist	
	Set up at church	Church, Florist, Planner	Bring music stands, just married gear, rice	
	Bride gets ready	Venue/Inn	Bride/bridesmaids	
	Rentals delivered	Venue	Rental Company	
	Cake is delivered	Venue	Baker	
2:00 pm	Photos	Venue/Inn	Bride/bridesmaids	
2:00 pm	Groom is taken to church	Church	Brother	
2:15 pm	Guests are picked up	Hotels	Transportation Company	
2:45 pm	Bride gets picked up	Venue/Inn		
3:00 pm	Wedding	Church	Flower petals white & cream to throw	Petals in Nantucket baskets / give to guests to throw
	Groom brings his mother down, exits and returns to front	Church	"Jesu, Joy"—Bach	

	Groom's sister/husband sits	Church		
	Bride bro/sis in, brother out	Church		
	Groom seats mom, Groom out	Church		
	Dad brings bouquet, sits	Church		
	Groom comes out and waits	Church		
	Dad brings bride	Church	"Trumpet Voluntary"—Clarke	
	Reading responsorial psalm	Church		
	Groom's brother-in-law and sister-in-law to bring the gifts up to the altar before communion	Church		
	Offertory	Church	"Sonata in C Major"—Corrette	
	Communion	Church	"Air on the G String"—Bach	
	Recessional	Church	"Scherzo" from Sonata in D Major—Offenbach	
	Vows, Exit, Toss Petals	Church		
	Exit, B & G go around and return to outside to greet guests	Church		
3:00 pm	Setup at Brandt Point	Brandt Point	Assistants, champagne reception	Bring glasses from rental company and supplies

4:00 pm	Band arrives	Venue	Band sets up	
4:00 pm	Transport to photos at Brandt Point Lighthouse	Photos at Brandt Point	Photographer	
	Guests are greeted with champagne, place shoes on straw mat, proceed to beach			
	After photos, guests can rinse feet in rose water, towel dry, and return to vans for transport to venue or walk back	Brandt Point		
	Sister gathers bouquets in Nantucket Basket	Brandt Point		
4:45 pm	Buses return	Venue		
	Sister gives basket to planner to place on tables	Brandt Point		
5:00 pm	Cocktails	Venue	Band	Band starts to play
6:30 pm	Dad will welcome, and ask priest to give blessing	Venue		
6:30 pm	Salad served	Venue		
7:00 pm	Entrees served	Venue		
7:45 pm	Announce that cake will be cut	Venue		
7:55 pm	Cut cake, wheeled away	Venue		
8:00 pm	First dance	Venue		Band announces Mr. & Mrs.

8:05 pm	Dance with parents	Venue		
8:15 pm	Cake gets passed, doors opened to side room	Venue		
8:15 pm	Dancing	Venue		
10:00 pm	Reception ends, guests continue at area venues	Venue		

Wedding Checklist

Pre-wedding-day events:
Formal Photos
Showers
Gentlemen's events
Ceremony rehearsals
Rehearsal dinner

Day-of-wedding preparation:
Hair
Makeup
Clothing (bridal party and guests of honor)
Rentals
Snacks

Ceremony:
Pre-ceremony customs
Officiant
Venue
Music ensemble
Bridal party
Florals
Rentals
Decor

Reception:

Decor

Florals

Entertainment

Photo session

Cocktail hour

Party introductions

First dance

Family dance

Specialized customs and reception traditions

Dinner/food

Cutting of the cake

Garter/bouquet toss

Socializing and dancing

Wedding party departure

Critical Elements of Every Wedding

While you will want to include the elements that are most important to your client, you may also need to educate them on wedding basics. The wedding checklist sidebar will give you a way to make sure all bases are covered. Your client may not be aware of the many players that could be involved to achieve the look they want for their special day. It's up to you to educate and guide them to get results that everyone will be proud of.

Theme and Concept Development

First, listen to your clients. Take note of their style and how they envision their event. Then add your "planner pizzazz" and offer suggestions to bring the wedding to a new level. Here is where you pull out all the stops and strut your stuff. While you must consider the wishes of the client, you should also show how you will carry out their dreams and desires at a new and exciting level. As a professional, you have access to many vendors who can help add an interesting and unique touch to their celebration. Don't be afraid to present your ideas, keeping in mind that they may want to keep things simple. Remember, it's their day, not yours!

Location

You may have several locations to work with—rehearsal dinner, ceremony, and reception, along with all the pre- and post-festivities as well. Create tabs or files on each and make sure you cover timing for setup and installation, teardown, and any other special rules or regulations the venues may have. Many churches don't allow a champagne toast on the sidewalk outside. Some venues will have hourly rates for setup outside the contracted rental time. Review your needs with all your venues and relay this information to your client so there are no surprises when the bill is submitted.

Guest List

The wedding guest list will most likely come from a variety of sources. If you are handling the mailing of the save-the-dates or invitations, you will want to start the process early. It's their party, so they can handle the invitation list as they wish, but remember that this can affect the planning when it comes to table seating and building capacities. Make sure you are aware of this and let your client know before they invite second and third cousins. Or, if they wish to expand the list, have an option ready to accommodate their needs.

Calling All Guests!

My clients (the parents of the bride) had booked their facility, a lovely old estate, with a seating capacity of 100 guests. As the planning ensued and the wedding began to take shape, the guest list expanded to include more than 100 attendees. We explored our options, which included an increase in rental fee, securing a tent to be installed near the estate, and creating decor to fill the tent that complemented the charming antique home. The end result was their daughter's dream wedding for all to see and enjoy (albeit, at a higher cost). Moral of the story: Listen, explore your options, and work to give them what they want. Get approval before spending, though, so everyone is aware of the additional price tag.

Cuisine

Hot dogs or filet mignon, plated or buffet, full seated dinner or buffet-style hors d'oeuvres . . . your recommendations should fit both your client's budget and their desires. Call on your favorite caterers or venues to help you bring the food experience to a new and unique level with interesting menus, presentations, or pairings of food and beverages. Signature drinks are a great way to personalize the bride and groom's special day. A gentlemen's cart with Dark and Stormys and cigars gives the groom his own festive part of the reception. Once again, ask about their style and favorites and call on your catering pros to help you shine!

Entertainment

This very important element—both during the wedding ceremony and at the reception—will naturally flow from the style and desires of the wedding couple. You can help them by offering suggestions for ceremony music, first dances, or even for music they will use for their wedding video. Staying on top of popular songs or calling on entertainment professionals to assist will help the decision-making process move along for the couple. The wedding budget may drive many of these selections, with live performances being more costly than a DJ or prerecorded selections. Give your client options and pricing and let them decide what will work best for them.

Pulling the Details Together

Decor and Rentals

The wedding theme will set the tone for your suggestions on decor and rental items. Budget also plays an important role. Be careful to understand the priorities of your client and offer suggestions that stay within their means. It's fine to offer high-, middle-, and low-end choices, giving them options so they can achieve the look they want without breaking the bank.

Tented and Outdoor Weddings

Tented weddings add a new level of planning skill and consideration to the wedding process. Permitting, identifying electrical needs, handling disposals, ordering rentals—these are just a sample of the additional planning tasks you will need to consider with a tented event. If it will be in a public area, the town must be notified and must provide approvals from the building and health departments. The fire department must approve any fabrics that will be used, and "burn" tests must be done to make sure they are fire-retardant. If you order fabric yourself, make sure you get this done beforehand, and have the necessary certificates to present to the fire marshal. Consider the effects of bad weather, placement of your tent, and, of course, make sure all the permits are in place well in advance. While a tent may be a necessity, it will also increase the cost of the wedding. In return for the investment, your client will get additional seating and peace of mind that the weather won't put a damper on their wedding day.

Recap

Although you may not conduct a formal evaluation of your wedding event, you will certainly want to debrief with the client and review what worked and what concerns they had. If you have had a strong production schedule and were lucky enough not to have to resort to contingency plans, you can feel assured that your event was a success. A formal evaluation with your client will help you with future weddings, and you will also be able to share this feedback with your vendors to improve both your, and their, services. Consider taking notes and even creating a checklist to review each of the wedding elements, including vendors' performance. This meeting might also be a time to present any wedding videos, photo albums, or thank-you notes that the client ordered. You may also have items to return from the wedding reception, such as serving utensils, champagne glasses, or the guestbook.

What It Costs

Planning tools (software for event time lines, guest list management, seating arrangements, contracts, and vendor lists): $299 and up

Ingredients for a proposal (scrapbook of past events with printed pictures and sample elements, DVD of photo montage, letters of recommendation, Microsoft Office PowerPoint Presentation): $100 to $300

Vendor samples (CD from wedding band, sample packets from linen company, calligrapher, invitation artist, the wedding cake designer, ice sculptor, and caterer): $100 and under

Frequently Asked Questions

1. *Should I help my clients set their budget, or simply provide ideas and costs and let them decide what they want to spend?*

   Quite often, when asked about a budget, a client will be unsure of what to set. Unfortunately, the budget helps you suggest the level of decor, types of food, or even the possible location. You may have a sample budget with price ranges for certain items to help a client come to terms with what they can afford. In your area, select low-, medium-, and high-priced venues and report on the associated catering costs. Give a sample menu for a $30-per-person meal, a $50-per-person meal, and then a $150-per-person meal. Present three levels of entertainment and a few ideas for floral choices. Insert the per-item costs into a budget and sum up the totals to show the final cost for each of the levels. Add in your hourly or percentage fees to give them an idea of what they could spend on their wedding celebration. Then leave it up to them to decide what they are comfortable committing to for an overall budget.

2. *I will only handle the day-of details. Is it necessary to know all the vendors and people involved?*

   Absolutely! If you will be required to line up the wedding party or consult with the chef, you should familiarize yourself with their names, what roles they will play, and any other special requests they or the bridal couple may have. It's also a good idea to confirm services before the wedding so you will avoid the stressful call when someone has not arrived. Even if the bride feels confident that all is confirmed, a personal call and introduction from you the week before is a great safety measure to ensure smooth sailing on the wedding day.

3. *How far ahead of time should I acquire my permits and licenses if I am coordinating a tented event?*

   The sooner the better! Sometimes it takes months for approvals if a town governing committee meets monthly or quarterly. If you need to call an organization like Dig Safe System, Inc. (www.digsafe.com, in New England) to inspect the tenting site, you will need to arrange this well in advance.

Fire departments will want to inspect any decor or flammables and may even prohibit candles or votives. If you don't gather this important information early enough, you may risk spending money on votive candles only to find you are unable to use them come the wedding day. A good rule of thumb is to get your approvals in writing sooner rather than later to save time and money during the planning process.

4. *How much information should I require from my vendors? Can I assume they will take care of all their own needs?*

Most vendors will come prepared to fulfill their obligations as promised. In some instances, they will expect you to have obtained all necessary permits (i.e., tent company), or have ordered extra power (i.e., lighting company providing pin spots on tables and up-lighting). You should ask them to provide a detailed list of their requirements, including permits, power, space, tables, setup and teardown time, food or hospitality needs (green room for entertainers, meals for staff, overnight rooms), or anything else they might need. If their contract is very simple, a phone call or meeting to review their needs is in order. Confirm details in advance, or you may face additional charges or embarrassment when the lights go out because of a limited power supply.

10 Unique Wedding Trends—The Old and the New

Weddings today come in many shapes and sizes. While the tradition of marriage is the reason behind the event, the setting, style, and individual event components are as varied as each of the couples saying "I do!" This chapter will cover some of the different choices folks may make for their wedding-day celebration. Appendix B also includes some Web sites that will direct the couple to more information on the wedding style of their choice. According to The Wedding Report, over half of all weddings today are traditional in style. While you will want to be familiar with traditional wedding styles, it's also a good idea to brush up on new trends so you can respond knowledgeably to their questions.

Client Profiles and Personalities

The personalities of your wedding clients will come in all shapes and sizes. You will have brides who will want to be involved in every flower selection and bow color and others that will say, "Whatever you suggest!" You may have multiple managers that you will have to negotiate with to come up with final decisions that everyone is happy with.

For the most extreme of clients, and those in between, the best advice is to listen, communicate clearly, and keep track—in writing—of all the details. If they ask for your advice, give it. Keep the budget in mind and try to offer suggestions that fit within these financial parameters. Don't show them photos of a million-dollar reception if they have a limited budget, unless you can present low-cost alternatives to get the same look without breaking the bank. If they want only the best, don't shop for supplies at the discount store. Purchase items that fit both their style and price point to deliver quality and fulfill their dreams for this special day.

Weddings are wonderful, emotional celebrations. As a planner, you get to enjoy the fun part—planning the festivities. The actual wedding event, though, is a small part of the very intense process of getting married. The reality of joining in the bonds of matrimony will mean two families will be coming together, one or both parties may be relocating, the bride or groom may be changing jobs, and life as a single person is coming to a screeching halt. Planning the wedding may require more decisions and compromises than the couple will have faced up to this point. The best and worse of their personalities (and their families') may surface. And as the planner, you may be caught in the middle. You also have the unique role of smoothing over the rough edges of these moments, helping to buffer the personalities of overzealous mothers-in-law and stressed-out brides. When things get tense, take a deep breath, let them air their thoughts, and then carefully continue with suggestions to help them reach their goal—a fabulous wedding day.

Tried and True

The main parts of the wedding celebration—the ceremony and reception—have some basic features that you may want to be aware of. Rules for getting a marriage license, the order of the wedding party during the procession, seating at the ceremony, and festivities at the reception are just a few of the many details you will need to advise your clients on. In the end, it's up to them to decide what they will include or leave out during their special day. There are some "must-dos"—like applying for the marriage license—that can't be avoided. Each state and country will have its own set of rules. Advise the couple to contact their local or state agency for the specifics. A good rule of thumb: Don't wait until the last minute.

Ceremony Basics

The order of the bridal party is another loosely followed custom (check out the sidebar for the traditional order). Typically, the groomsmen will assist in seating guests, although this can vary depending on the religious denomination of the ceremony. Nowadays there is much more flexibility with the seating rules, and guests can often choose the side they wish to sit on. The couple will have the first rows set aside for the bridal party and family, but after that, it's often first come, first served. Let the couple decide how formal or informal they want the seating to be.

Other elements of the ceremony may include music, a program booklet, candle lighting, readings, and the exchange of vows. The music may include a prelude, processional for the bridal party, music for the bride, music during the service, and, of course, the festive recessional. Ceremony music choices should be discussed with the music liturgist prior to the wedding. The program booklet gives a chance for the couple to recognize key people and outline the schedule of the service. Other unique elements of the ceremony may include a candle lighting, special poems or prayers for loved ones, or a post-ceremony butterfly release outside the church. Many places discourage the tossing of rice or rose petals, so it's best to check with the person in charge before tossing away. There are bird-safe tossing pellets available online or at bridal supply stores that will let you keep the tradition without harming the environment. As a planner, you may want to be prepared to tidy up afterward to keep the couple on good terms with their house of worship.

The Reception

The festivities after the ceremony typically include a welcoming of the guests by the couple, dining, and dancing. The greeting of the guests by the bride and groom can be in the form of a reception line held at the ceremony location or reception site. The line can include the bridal party, family members, or other guests of honor. Other customs may include the tossing of the bouquet and the garter, cake cutting, first dances, and the couple's farewell. All of these are optional elements and personal

Traditional Wedding Procession

Grandparents of the groom

Grandparents of the bride

Mother of the groom (and father, or he can be already be seated)

Mother of the bride

Groomsmen (if they are waiting at the altar with the groom)

Bridesmaids (process alone or with groomsmen)

Maid of honor

Ring bearer

Flower girl

Bride and escort (father, both parents, escort of choice)

choices made by the couple. As a planner, you should be ready to help coordinate the flow of the reception and the timing of the elements that are most important to the couple.

Religious Ceremonies and Cultural Customs

Many couples will want to have a religious component to their wedding. You will want to understand the rules and regulations of the place of worship and abide by its requests for a smooth ceremony. You may be required to present payment on behalf of the couple to any parties involved, such as the officiant, organist, music director, or assistants (i.e., altar servers). It's best to verify your list of details and on-site personnel well before the event. Consider timing of other services, rules regarding alcohol, rice, or confetti throws, as well as floral and decor treatments that the couple may want to bring in. Even if the couple has already discussed the details with the coordinator at the place of worship, it's always best to go over the details so nothing is left out. Let's take a look at some specific elements of religious ceremonies you will want to be aware of.

Catholic Weddings

Marriages in the Catholic faith will require that the ceremony be held at a church. As soon as the couple decides they will have a Catholic wedding ceremony, they should meet with their parish priest to discuss available dates and any pre-wedding preparations they will need to make. As a planner, you won't need to be too involved with this, but it's good to advise the couple to make the necessary contacts to understand the process. The ceremony itself can be a full Mass, which could last an hour, or a marriage outside the Mass, which is a shorter service and does not have all the elements of a full Mass. It's best to have the couple discuss their wishes with their parish priest or liaison. Selections of music, timing, and readings can be made and approved in advance. The rehearsal will allow the bridal party, priest, and readers to review the process for a smooth wedding day. A program booklet, which you may be asked to create, will also allow you to confirm the flow of the ceremony and the order of activities.

Protestant Celebrations

Protestant services, while similar to a Catholic service, have a biblical focus and are more flexible with readings, music, timing, location of the ceremony, and other features of the celebration. There are many resources (like www.foreverwed.com and www.kingdomquest.com) that offer suggestions on wedding elements and accessories. They also have online planning tools available. Compare these with what you currently use to make sure you aren't missing any details.

When it comes to details like the processional and seating of guests, many couples are relaxing the traditional standard of seating the bride's family on the left (upon entering the church) and the groom's to the right. Typically space will be set aside at the front of the ceremony venue for the wedding party and guests of honor. Check out the sidebar for tips on lining up the bridal party. There is much more flexibility as to location with Protestant services, with ceremonies being held outdoors or in other interesting locations.

Jewish Weddings

Weddings celebrated in the Jewish faith include features such as signing the ketubah, a marriage contract signed by both bride and groom formalizing their wedding commitment, and the use of a huppah, a lovely canopy created for the bridal couple to stand under during the ceremony. Gentlemen are required to wear a yarmulke, a small covering for their head. The tradition of the groom stepping on a wineglass is typically performed after the vows and has many meanings. Some say it symbolizes the fragility of human happiness; others feel it reminds the couple of the destruction of the temples of Jerusalem. Seating during the ceremony is customarily with the groom's family to the left of the altar (as guests enter from the rear) and the bride's family to the right. Both parents will often walk the bride down the aisle. During the reception a special dance may be included where the bridal couple is carried on chairs to the dance floor surrounded by guests and family.

Cultural Touches

Today's couples may want to honor their heritage by adding cultural customs to their wedding. Here are a few tips on adding these international touches to your client's celebrations:

- African—"Jumping the broom" at the reception symbolizes the start of the couple's new life together. Cowrie shells, a sign of purity and beauty, are often used for decor elements.
- Armenian—The phrase "May you grow old on one pillow" is used in print pieces for these weddings.

- Chinese—A traditional tea ceremony with the bride serving her parents is customary. The groom can also be involved, serving to his family. Red is a favorite color; a symbol of celebration and prosperity. The bridal couple will want to visit each table for a toast.
- Dutch—A "wish tree" branch is set up by the couple's table at the reception. Guests write a message on a paper leaf and present it to the couple to read and place on the tree branch.
- French—The groom walks his mother down the aisle and then awaits the arrival of his bride.
- German—Breaking items and cleaning up the mess symbolizes the couple's ability to face the trials of marriage together.
- Greek—The bride and groom are treated as king and queen wearing crowns made of orange blossoms.
- Indian—Marigolds are a floral favorite in Indian weddings. The sprinkling of petals over the couple by the groom's brother is thought to prevent evil from touching the couple's new marriage. These weddings can be multiday affairs and include painting the bride's hands and feet with intricate henna designs and the use of many flowers for garlands and decor.
- Irish—Some of the symbols of an Irish wedding include the traditional claddagh wedding ring and a horseshoe for the bride to bring good luck, sometimes tied to her bouquet. Others include the love knot, the harp, and the four-leaf clover. Shamrocks can be used in floral decor for reception tables. No Irish wedding would be complete without a guest's performance of a song or poem with the word "love" in it to elicit a kiss from the wedding couple.
- Italian—Jordan almonds are favorite party favors, symbolizing the combination of bitterness and sweetness in their lives together as a married couple.
- Japanese—Nine sips of sake represent the new bond of husband and wife—three from each of three cups representing the family couples (bride and groom and parents) and three human flaws (hatred, passion, and ignorance).
- Korean—Animals that mate for life are used in these weddings, including ducks and geese, to symbolize the couple's fidelity.
- Mexican—The traditional piñata is still a party favorite. Guests will also form a heart-shaped circle around the couple before their first dance. The

custom of the groom presenting thirteen coins to his bride represents Jesus and his apostles. A mariachi band is a typical entertainment choice as well.

- Polish—A crown of rosemary leaves, which is worn by the bride, is a sign of remembrance.
- Scottish—Bagpipes are an entertainment favorite for Scottish weddings, especially during the processional. If the groom is Scottish, he may also present the bride with his clan's tartan sash to welcome her into his family.
- Swedish—A silver coin from her dad and gold coin from her mom, worn in the bride's left and right shoe, symbolizes her never going without.
- Turkish—Before the wedding, the single girls sign the soles of the bride's shoes, allowing the bride to see who will marry next. At the end of the night, the person whose name is most faded will be the next to walk down the aisle.

When working with a couple, let them decide what elements of their religion or culture they will want to incorporate into their celebration. More often than not, it will be a combination of the tried and true with elements reflecting their own personal style. More important, you will want to focus on the differences and nuances they want to add and use your skill and industry knowledge to source out the vendors or suppliers needed to make it happen.

Communication Is Key

It will be imperative to understand the chain of command for each of your clients. In some cases, the bride and groom will be the sole decision makers. When you meet with the couple to begin the planning, you will want to ask them who else should be involved in the decision-making process, or at least be updated as the planning progresses. How should information be presented, and who is the ultimate decision maker? There will be financial implications attached to every selection that's made, so don't forget to cover your bases by following up in writing and getting approvals on all orders placed. It's not unusual for a client to get caught up in the planning moment as you present your creative ideas and bring their wedding to a new level. This is an exciting and emotional time, but don't forget your fiscal responsibility to those footing the bill. Temper the enthusiasm as the wedding takes on a life of its own with deposits and contracts, and you will be earning your keep as a professional planner.

Unique Wedding Trends

Destination Weddings

One of the most popular trends in weddings today is the destination wedding. According to the Library of Congress, Business Reference Service, one in ten weddings is held in a location other than the bride's or groom's hometown. Couples that are attracted to planning a destination wedding are often older, both working, and well traveled, and see their wedding as a chance to celebrate in an exotic or special resort area. A destination wedding will not have the same invitation acceptance rate, as a locally held wedding, as they are more costly for the guests to participate in. They may be smaller in size but will often have more activities to coordinate and can last several days—more reasons to hire a pro to pull the details together.

Here's a look at a planning time line leading up to a destination wedding I planned on Nantucket Island for a couple living in Washington, D.C. The initial telephone conversation was one year prior to their wedding date. A personal visit was made one month later. This schedule covers some of the many details that were discussed and reviewed during the months of planning. An additional peek at a production schedule for the day before activities began will give you a sense of how complex the planning around the actual wedding day can be.

Planning Timetable for Destination Wedding

Month	Activities			
	Week 1	Week 2	Week 3	Week 4
January	Bride: guest list to Jill			
		B & G: (bride & groom) sign venue contract		send check to venue
			Planner: save-the-date card	
				Planner: calligraphy for invitation

Month	Activities			
	Week 1	Week 2	Week 3	Week 4
	Planner: photographer recommendations			
		Music for wedding: strings		
			Music for reception: send demo tapes	Contract sent to BSO cellist
	Planner: contract for florals			
February	Save-the-dates ordered			
		Book transportation on ferry (B/G/Planner)		
			Contract sent to photographer	
				Contract sent to florist
		Samples requested from calligrapher		
			Sample coming for invitation	
March	Wedding venue		rehearsal dinner venue	
	Save-the-dates sent		Menu, setup, timing	
		tent, rentals, florals, menu		
	Floral discussion		entertainment	
	Cake research			

Month	Activities			
	Week 1	Week 2	Week 3	Week 4
	See revisions on photographer's contract			
		Invitations: final decisions		
	Entertainment timing and booking			
April	Transportation	Rental Selections		Visit the island
	Florals	Rental orders placed	Appointments with Wedding Venue	
	Discussion on setup and design		Chef at Rehearsal Dinner Venue	
	Explore linen, rental options		Visit rental company, church	
		Finalize design and theme (venues)		Visit hotels/inns
	Informal photos taken		Appointments with salon	
	Cake sampling			
May	Invitations are sent	Menu selections		Confirm vendors
	Arrange transportation			
	Choose music			
			Decide on themed amenities (napkins, favors, etc.)	

Month	Activities			
	Week 1	Week 2	Week 3	Week 4
	Decide on services and make appointments			
		Decide on cake vendor and order		
June	Bride/Groom conference call			
		Planner to check progress with vendors		
			Planner to order gifts, amenities	
				Printing of additional items (program booklet/menus)
	Purchase and prep of any custom decor			
		Coordination of permitting		
July			Bride provides seating arrangements	
				Planner to give final numbers to venues
		Details of decor with florist		

Month	Activities			
	Week 1	Week 2	Week 3	Week 4
	Gather necessities: rings, gifts, clothing			
August	Receipt of final personalized items			
		Planner to develop production schedules		
			Calls and follow up with all vendors	
				Final arrangements made

Day-Before Schedule

Time	Activity	Action
9:00 am	Tent setup	Tent company
9:00 am	Drop girls at beach to set up/hold space	4 Assistants: towels, Wiffle bat/ball, bocci, lacrosse sticks, horseshoes
10:00 am	Transportation to beach	Host facility or island transportation
10:30 am	Pick up order at bakery	
11:00 am	Drop sandwiches/coolers at beach	Assistants to help
11:30 am	Ladies luncheon	Check with restaurant
12 Noon	Setup for rehearsal dinner	Planner with assistants at venue
2:00 pm	Hair, bride	Salon on Main Street
2:30 pm	Pick up guys at beach	Island transportation
3:00 pm	Island transportation delivery	Planner to deliver refreshments for the bus ride to venue (cooler of beer / Jenn martinis / water / straws in tins), bows and signage
3:45 pm	Pick up bride, take to church	Planner

Time	Activity	Action
4:00 pm	Musician and friend to SH	P/u at airport or get after rehearsal
4:00 pm	Rehearsal at church	Groom, bride, and family
4:45 pm	B & G back to hotel to change	
4:45 pm	Planner to venue	Pick up musicians / check setup / band equipment / light candles
5:10 pm	P/u at Hotel 1	Bus One can depart H1 at 5:15 pm for venue
5:20 pm	P/u at Hotel 2	Bus Two can go to H3 for overflow, then to venue
5:10 pm	P/u at Hotel 3	Bus Three can depart H3 at 5:10 pm
5:20 pm	P/u at Hotel 4	Bus Four can depart H1 at 5:20 pm, go to H2 at 5:30 pm
6:00 pm	Arrive at venue	Planner
	Guests move to lawn area	
	Speech/toast	Father of bride to start
	Priest to do blessing	Father John
10:00 pm	Dinner ends	Buses to town

Location, location, location

Throwing a wedding at an unusual location can be a treat for everyone. Disney just launched Disney's Fairy Tale Weddings (www.disneyweddings.com); although they come with some on-site planning assistance, clients still may need a professional to pull the details together. Consider locations that welcome unique activities such as hot air ballooning, bungee jumping, or white-water rafting. The sky's the limit, so if you have an adventurous couple, let them push you out of your comfort zone and test your planning prowess by pulling together an unusual celebration.

Multiday events

Weddings held at unique and exclusive locations will often mean that guests will plan a few extra days for their trip to make the travel worth their while. They may view the destination wedding as a mini-vacation. The couple may want to consider hosting additional events depending on when folks will be arriving. Additional events that all guests can and should be invited to include the welcome reception, rehearsal dinner, or post-wedding brunch. Specialized events for the wedding party and guests include luncheons, golf, fishing or beach events, or any tour that is appropriate for the location, perhaps at a winery or museum. These extra events will require additional planning time, so discuss this with your client to determine how involved they will want you to be.

Who pays

As with any other wedding, there are many ways to fund these events. While tradition has the bride's family hosting the wedding and the groom's family, the rehearsal dinner, couples today are getting more involved with funding some of the events, especially if they are both working and are selecting something a bit out of the ordinary. A welcome reception might be hosted by a family member or close family friend. A bridal luncheon can be hosted by the bridesmaids, especially if many of the guests were not able to attend a bridal shower. The gentlemen's activities—whether a day at the beach or a day on the golf course—can be paid for by the groomsmen or the groom. There is nothing set in stone for hosting these events. It depends on the couple, their financial situation, and the support they get from family and friends during the planning process. If you are asked to deal with someone outside the contract (bride/groom/family hosting), just make sure you discuss your involvement and any cost for the time you spend to coordinate an additional event for the couple.

If the destination is an international location, the couple (or you) may want to open a checking account in the city where the wedding will be held in order to expedite payment for services. Exchange rates and banking customs can also have an impact on the orders you place and the timeliness of deliveries, so investigate ahead of time to avoid disappointment.

Transportation

Getting the bridal couple to their wedding destination is one logistical consideration. There's also the wedding and bridal party attire, attendant gifts, any decor or personalized items like guestbook, favors, programs, or welcome gifts. As you can imagine, planning for the cost as well as the safe and timely arrival of items is critical. The bride may want to bring her dress on the airplane with her to avoid any "lost baggage" disasters. Some elements may be handled at the destination location, if available. This will require additional coordination on the planner's part, and possibly extra days on-site to source out the suppliers and pull the local details together. Don't forget to figure these into your budget to get compensated for your time and travel expenses.

Timing is everything

Planning a destination wedding should begin at least a year in advance. Since guests will be asked to make more of a financial and time commitment to attend a destination wedding, an early reminder in the form of a save-the-date card is imperative. Guests will need to plan time off from work and set aside extra funds to pay for travel and accommodation expenses that are typically not part of a local wedding.

The engaged couple will also have to consider the overall impact a destination wedding will have on their guests, and balance the extravagance of their location with the feasibility of their guests being able to attend. Encourage the couple to take an honest look at the likelihood of a favorable response from the majority of their guest list. It wouldn't be a festive occasion if only a few can afford the time and travel expense. Perhaps the trip to Fiji can be saved for the honeymoon! On the other hand, a destination wedding allows for a smaller, more intimate gathering and can serve as a getaway for not only the bridal couple but also their family and closest friends. If notice is given well in advance, guests may forgo their annual vacation to attend a destination wedding.

Permits and licensing

Getting approvals and licenses may take more time, so encourage your couple to start early. Check with local state offices for individual requirements. International locations could have different requirements, so encourage the couple to plan early and cover all their legal bases. If international travel will be required, remind the couple to update their visa or passport and take any necessary medical precautions for safe and trouble-free travel.

Extras

Hosting a party in an unfamiliar location brings its own set of challenges. Guests with small children will not have their favorite babysitter on hand to care for little ones while the reception celebration is in full swing. Consider assisting your client by coordinating babysitting services, putting together a list of activities for families or couples, or sharing favorite spots for spa services. A welcome bag with a booklet of suggestions or services will make guests feel right at home and leave a lasting impression of your attention to detail.

Bridal Couple Web Sites

Many couples will develop their own personal Web site for the wedding to share information and details. While this won't replace the formal invitation to the wedding or related parties, it's a good way to list information on hotels, travel, directions, excursions, and their gift registry. Check out chapter 11 for more information on becoming e-savvy. If the couple will rely on you for help in this area, make sure you estimate your time and expertise and add this service as a line item in your contract.

Green Weddings

For those couples concerned with the environment and sensitive to the green cause, help them to work elements into their wedding day that are cost-, fuel-, and energy-efficient. Areas where you can be environmentally friendly include choice in serviceware, linens, centerpieces, food, fashion, and use of electricity or disposal procedures.

Here are a few green tips:

- Use green invitations; use recycled paper or natural products for decor or favors.
- Don't use plastics; consider china. Use bamboo or some other recyclable serviceware.
- Design with plantables. Choose living plants to top your tables. Let guests take them home to replant in their gardens or yards.
- Use the old instead of the new; consider vintage clothing or tablecloths; use hemp or cotton as fabric choices.
- Eat organic! Find an organic-focused caterer. Ask your venue to prepare environmentally friendly foods. Use local vendors for fresh foods and to cut down on transportation costs, saving fuel and preventing damage to the environment.
- Planned tossing; recycle trash. Have separate refuse containers to toss away trash. Compost if you can.

- Travel green. Suggest transportation methods that go easy on the environment. Plan the ceremony and reception at adjacent locations so guests can walk from one to the other. Local vendors will eliminate fuel consumption.

Check out Appendix B for a list of resources to further help your clients with their green wedding.

Weddings from the Heart

For the couple who wishes to share their good fortune with those who are less privileged, or with their favorite charities, there are many ways to direct gift giving to the charity of their choice. If you help them develop their Web site, you can post their wish to have guests donate to a charity rather than give a personal gift, and add the links directly to the wedding Web site. To accomplish the goal of a combination green and philanthropic wedding theme, direct guests to donate to the World Wildlife Fund or the Rainforest Alliance. One of my clients asked guests to make a local donation at the Massachusetts Society for the Prevention of Cruelty to Animals (www.mspca.org) in lieu of gifts, and pets were even part of the guest list! You can research the local chapter to assist your couples in making a pet friendly donation for their favors at www.spca.com.

Consider delivering leftover food to a local food bank or a homeless shelter. A home for elders would welcome leftover wedding florals or favors as an added treat for their residents. A bride and her party might consider donating their wedding attire to a women's organization that could pass them on to those less fortunate.

Here are a few ways to steer your charity-minded client in the right direction:

1. List your favorite charity (or charities) on the wedding Web site.
2. Specify the stores you would like them to purchase a wedding gift from that will give a percentage to charity.
3. Print a card for each place setting that lists your charity of choice.
4. Locate a retailer that donates as you purchase. Carlson Craft (www.carlson craft.com) and eInvite.com will donate 10 to 15 percent of your invitation purchase to charity.
5. Carlson Wagonlit Travel will donate 5 percent of your honeymoon cost to charity.
6. Check out the I DO foundation at www.idofoundation.org for more ideas to

share with your clients. They will even help the wedding couple build a Web site that will make giving easier for guests.

Same-Sex Weddings

Internationally, Canada, Belgium, the Netherlands, Norway, South Africa, and Spain all welcome the marital bliss of gay couples. With the recent rulings in Massachusetts, and Connecticut, recognizing the legality of same-sex marriages, a new focal area of wedding planning has surfaced in the United States. If you find yourself with a gay or lesbian client, make sure you check on the legal details in your state to formalize this ceremony. The Web site for Gay & Lesbian Advocates & Defenders (www.glad.org) has information and updates on state regulations for gay and lesbian marriages, including waiting periods, changing surnames, and legally performing the ceremony. In terms of design and decor, defer to the style and personalities of the couple to settle on thematic elements that are on target to create a unique wedding experience. Check out this Web site for updates on regulations around the world: http://gaylife.about.com/od/samesexmarriage/a/legalgaymarriage.htm.

What It Costs

Payment on behalf of the couple to officiant, organist, music director or assistants: $50 to $300 per person

Book or Web site guides on wedding ceremonies and etiquette: $10 to $50 each

Marriage license: $20 to $100

Traveling to a destination wedding in Aruba (three nights at a hotel, airfare, rental car/van, meals): $1,000 to $1,500 per couple

Planning in Aruba (international phone calls, shipping supplies beforehand, exchanging currency): $3.99 a month plus $ .54 a minute (international plan), $100 to $500 for shipping supplies

Special skill sets (butterfly release course, sewing machine, classes on floral design, calligraphy set, becoming ordained to perform marriage ceremonies, and becoming a Carlson Craft dealer): $350 and up

Passport (official pictures and application fee): $120

Frequently Asked Questions

1. *How can I make a very traditional wedding more unique for my clients?*
   Consider their style and use your flair to take it to the next level. You can
   incorporate thematic elements into their aisle runner with monogramming,
   or update the traditional rice toss with a butterfly release. Let their style
   drive how far you can push a traditional couple toward creating a once-in-
   a-lifetime experience for everyone.

2. *I have signed on a client for a destination wedding. Now they want me to
   plan another four events during their wedding weekend. How can I price my
   services for this?*
   Treat each event as a separate project and add in your time and the
   expenses associated with the planning process. Make sure your original
   contract clearly states the parameters of your services. You should specify
   the wedding-related services you will provide, such as venue and vendor
   selection, contracting, and execution. If they have added a welcome reception, perhaps the expenses won't increase much (you will already be on-
   site at the destination), but your time to coordinate invitations, menu, and
   decor for this event should be charged as services outside the contract.
   Time is money, so don't be afraid to charge for it.

3. *I have been asked to assist with a same-sex wedding. Are there any trends
   I should incorporate?*
   Often couples will want to play up their unique relationship and dress in
   festive drag, both wearing formal men's wear or both in formal gowns.
   Anything goes! Some favorite decor elements include rainbow-colored
   cakes, purple anything, or ultra chic with all black-and-silver-studded
   appointments. As with any client, you will want to match their personality
   and style to truly make it their special day. Whether they are private, shy,
   outgoing, or casual, let them steer you in the direction they are most comfortable with.

4. *Recycled products can look a little rustic. What kind of "green" treatments*

can we incorporate into the design while still ensuring that the wedding will look elegant?

Try beeswax candles; they are just like regular ones and come in different shapes. You can tuck them into glass holders to add a punch of color to their natural honey tint. Also consider static or "chasing" battery-operated LED lights, which are low-energy and ecofriendly (http://www.lights4fun.co .uk). You can put them in florals, tuck them under sheer-colored hemp or gauze linens, or hang them from branches set in the center of tables. Use smooth black river rocks for an elegant look. Consider donating leftovers to a food kitchen or using glass instead of disposable plastic for serviceware. Every little bit counts!

E-Commerce and Internet Use

Using the Internet as a tool to grow and support your business is not only smart, but these days, it's imperative. Even in the high-touch field of wedding planning, it's important to root your creativity with some well-grounded tools. Web site development for your company and your clients, using the Internet to find vendors and clients, and visiting Web sites to stay abreast of wedding trends and basic planning information are all stops along the information highway you should plan to make. Let's start by considering how you'll market your business using technology.

Starting and Running Your Business

The Internet can provide loads of information to help you launch your business. Tools on writing a business plan, developing marketing materials, and researching for professionals to assist you are all a click away. Check out Appendix B for some sites that can help you get started.

Managing Your Finances Online

An easy way to streamline your finances is to link your bank account to your financial program. Many banks offer Internet banking and allow you to download transactions, pay bills, and accept payments from clients online. This will help you to streamline your bookkeeping and help with monthly reconciliations and management of your cash flow.

Applying for Special Status with State Agencies

Spend some time online researching opportunities that will give you special status as a business owner. For example, if you are a minority or a woman in Massachusetts, you can apply for status as an approved vendor by the State

Office of Minority and Women Business Assistance at www.somwba.state.ma.us/. This allows certified vendors to participate in affirmative action opportunities and obtain leads on business available only to certified companies. Various federal agencies offer contracting opportunities to specific businesses to encourage commerce by small or minority-owned businesses. Start with the Office of Small and Disadvantaged Business Utilization (www.osdbu.dot.gov) to check opportunities. You will find links to other opportunities on this site such as the link for woman-owned small businesses. The Minority Business Development Agency (www.mbda.gov) is another place to check for contracting opportunities.

Becoming an Online Resource

Just as you will use the Internet to source out vendors, suppliers, and ideas, you will also want your clients to be able to find you easily online. Over 84 percent of wedding couples use the Internet as a resource for planning their wedding (The Wedding Report, www.theweddingreport.com)—a great reason for you to be Internet-savvy. If you want your wedding planning business to pop up when couples are searching online, you need to be visible on the Internet. You can do this by creating your own Web site, writing and posting articles, being in the news, speaking at local events, and by posting helpful information or presentations online. A Web professional can help you with the behind-the-scenes details of increasing your online presence. In the meantime, don't be afraid to put yourself out there for all to see. If you enter a local contest for best services in the area, even if you aren't a winner, you will gain visibility by being listed as a contestant. Although these marketing tools are inexpensive, they do take some time to manage.

Web-Site Basics to Market Your Company

While there are many wedding specialty sites on which you can advertise, some for a fee and some at no cost, having your own Web site is crucial if you hope to market yourself effectively. The first step is to purchase your domain name. You can hire someone to help you with this who will then move on to design your site for you. The other option is to do your own research for a domain purchase and hosting services, and then to purchase a "shell" and build the Web site yourself. The first option is more costly, and it will take a certain amount of time to communicate your style and content to your webmaster; the latter, while cheaper, will be much more time-consuming. If you are not computer-savvy or interested in learning the basics and keeping your site updated, I highly recommend that you hire a professional to assist you. Having a site that is unprofessional-looking, outdated, or hard to navigate won't convince prospects to hire you as their wedding planner.

Pros and Cons to Being Your Own Webmaster

Do it yourself	Hire a pro
More economical	More expensive
Can update frequently	More costly to update
More time-consuming to update	Takes less time to update
Simpler in design	Web site is more detailed and unique in style and look
Longer learning curve in understanding search-engine complexities	A professional will help drive your Web site to the top of search engines
Time-consuming	Time-effective

Organizing Your Site

To start your site, make sure you have a simple yet effective home page that will clearly communicate your style and what you do. At the very least, have a tab for contact information, facts about your company, testimonials from satisfied customers, and sample descriptions of weddings you have created (with photos). Consider adding a news or blog page if you can manage to keep it up.

If you think you would want folks to purchase any items, you can consider adding a secure system such as PayPal (www.paypal.com) for accepting credit card payments. There are fees associated with these services, so consider how often you will use them and if they are worth the extra cost.

Web-Site Extras

Consider developing an "ask the pro" area of your Web site. Update it monthly with suggestions on wedding planning or how to work with vendors. Offer special packages or incentives for new clients. Run your own contests or promotions to draw visitors to your site. If you have a business relationship with a local bank, advertise your company and your Web site at a local branch to get your name out there.

E-Newsletters

Build a database and send a monthly newsletter to share ideas, photos of recent events, or planning and design tips. Work with your vendors to pull together ideas for floral designs, tablecloth trends, or venue suggestions. Ask your friends to forward them to anyone who may be interested. Even if some of your ideas are used by others, you are still getting your name and your creative energy out into the public eye and building your wedding planning reputation.

Helping Your Clients Get and Stay Connected

By developing a strong Internet presence you will also be helping your clients stay connected to you and to the planning process. Besides sourcing out the wedding details, they may also want to be linked to their guests to make attending their wedding a simple and enjoyable treat.

Couple Web Sites

Here's a list of sites that help the bride and groom to develop their own Web site. Many couples will want to take this project on by themselves, but if not, you can offer this as an added service. Some of these online resources will offer more than just a Web site, also providing tips on planning and tracking the wedding details. You should work with the couple to complement these additional features with your own planning tools. If anything, it will further remind them of critical deadlines and the many details that you will be managing for them.

www.eWedding.com
www.sitepride.com
www.webwedding.com
www.weddingtracker.com
www.weddingwebsites.com
www.wedshare.com

The couple's Web site can include photos and information on travel, gift giving, accommodations, schedules, and other events that may be happening to celebrate the wedding. Any excursions that the couple may plan should be listed with options to sign up, pay for any fees, or contact other attendees. For destination weddings, information on the wedding location is always helpful for guests and can include weather, travel tips, points of interest, and special events happening in the area around the time of the wedding. Weddingwebsites.com compares an array of Website providers and a discussion forum. SitePride.com even focuses on same-sex wedding Web sites.

Special Requests from the Heart

For couples that wish to encourage donations instead of gift giving, online communication makes it easy for guests to support the couple's favorite charities. Here are a few to suggest to your philanthropically minded couple:

www.changingthepresent.org/weddings
www.idofoundation.org
www.ourbiggivewedding.com
www.worldwildlife.org/weddings

Finding Suppliers for Your Weddings

Use the Internet to find unique and personalized products for your clients. Search engines like Google and Yahoo give hundreds of options for resources. Don't forget to go directly to the source, such as chocolate suppliers or candle companies. Personalized M&Ms for the bridal couple can be found at www.mymms.com. The NJ Candle company offers unscented votive candles in a wide array of colors. Carlson Craft offers monogrammed napkins, memo books, or matchbooks. You will want to become registered as a dealer, which will give you access not only to wedding favors but also to invitations and other printables. Register online at the www.carlsoncraft .com site.

Here is a list of suppliers for wedding items:

www.carlsoncraft.com
www.custom-chocolate.com
www.foreverwed.com
www.mymms.com
www.njcandle.com
www.weddingmountain.com
www.wherebridesgo.com

Staying on Top of Wedding Basics and Trends

The Internet is a great way to stay on top of trends. Even if you enjoy flipping through monthly magazines such as InStyle, Special Events, and BizBash, their online alternatives will give you a quick glimpse of what's hot and trendy. Other wedding sites such as The Knot or InStyle Weddings will feature celebrity or high-profile weddings that showcase top industry trends. Blogging, much like a diary of comments, ideas, and events, is another great way to keep up with issues, ideas, and challenges that other planners are having. Here are a few Web sites and blog locations that are fun to read and will keep you on your planning tiptoes!

www.aboutweddings.com
www.bestweddingblogs.com
www.bizbash.com
www.instyleweddings.com
www.mywedding.com/blogs/mywed
http://parisianevents.com/parisianparty
www.theknot.com
www.weddingblogawards.com

What It Costs

Domain name: $70 to $250

Web site help-sites (like godaddy.com) with up to five pages: $47.50 a month for 12 months

Webmaster: $50 to $200 an hour, $100 to $2,000 per service

PayPal option on Web site: $2.20 to $3.30 for every $100 (no start-up or monthly fees)

Being a member on an Internet site like The Knot or The Wedding Channel: Free to access for ideas and resources

Advertising on regional wedding sites (www.mywedding.com): $300 to $700 a year

Listing on The Wedding Zone with over 75,000 unique visitors per month: as low as $7.50/month

When it comes to being Internet-savvy, take it slowly, but don't ignore the importance of getting connected. Something is better than nothing. Clear, simple communication, done professionally, will put your company and identity on the Web for all to see. You can always update your site with additional features or try a new e-marketing technique as your confidence and time allows.

Frequently Asked Questions

1. *Should I have a Web site if I've only planned one wedding?*
   Traditional print methods of advertising such as the Yellow Pages, newspapers, magazines, or direct mailers are being overshadowed by electronic advertising. Search engines like Google and Yahoo are frequently used by customers looking for products and services. Accessibility via the World Wide Web will keep you at your customers' fingertips. I would recommend launching your Web site alongside your business and not waiting until you have a large portfolio to get things started. Begin with basic facts on what you do and how customers can reach you. Add a page of testimonials from happy clients and photos when you have them to show your talent and style!

2. *When I was planning my wedding, I saw many wedding planners listed on sites like www.theknot.com. As a planner who's just starting out, would you recommend that I pay their advertising fees, or should I take advantage of less-expensive alternatives?*
   There are many options for online advertising. Some are with national companies that welcome everyone, and others are regional with varying levels of visibility. Before you decide, you should ask the following questions: How many hits do they get from searches? How easy will it be for you to stand out from the crowd? How many other planners are also featured on the site? If you are one of a thousand wedding planners listed alphabetically and your company is Zebra Weddings, you won't get much business. If you specialize in destination weddings and there are only three featured, it may be a good place to put your advertising dollars. If you can be a preferred

vendor and submit an article on wedding ideas, visitors to the site will view you as a pro and give you a call.

3. *On top of starting a wedding planning company, I also make and sell personalized baked goods. Should I link the Web sites together or keep my two businesses separate?*

    If you can provide an additional service to your clients, and it's wedding-related, it would be fine to provide the link on your site, or make it an option if the item fits into their wedding plans. Many planners provide stationery services or unique gift items as part of their company's resources. You will want to keep both businesses professional and ensure that your clients don't feel you are spending too much time with the other business and not enough time planning their wedding.

4. *My company's name (Spectacular Events) is already being used as a domain (www.spectacularevents.com). Should I tweak my company's name or come up with a domain name that is similar?*

    This can be a challenge for potential clients when they do an Internet search for your business and reach a different company. It's a great company name, but if they find someone else, it's all for naught. You can try to buy the domain name (could be expensive) or alter your name slightly (The Spectacular Event Company or Spectacular Events by Ellen). Just make sure you purchase the domain name before you go through the expense and time of updating your documents and marketing materials to the new name.

Being the Best

Your excitement about wedding planning shows that you have a passion for the industry. As important as it is, passion alone will not allow you to build and grow a successful wedding planning business. You will need to complement your natural skills with other important talents to grow a successful wedding planning business.

Special events have been going on since the beginning of time. The Wedding at Cana, contests and competitions in the Roman Colosseum, the Olympics—I am sure you can think of numerous gatherings and celebrations that have occurred throughout the ages. While the event producers in 200 BC did not have degrees and certifications, they certainly had basic planning skills and acumen for event design and coordination. Today you need much more than a knack for event planning. The legal implications of an event gone awry are too great a risk for an unprepared enthusiast to take. The wedding planning process can be full of challenges, but with the right tools and training, they can be met with safe solutions. There are places to go for formal training to help you build your skills for a rewarding and exciting career in special events.

Formal Education

In chapter 1, I talked about the basic skills you will need to run your business. While it may not be necessary to get an MBA, it's not a bad idea to take some business courses. They will certainly help you to run your business in a professional way and will save you time and money in the long run. Consider complementing your business skill development with courses on event or wedding planning. Currently there are degree programs throughout the United States and internationally for special events planning and execution. Many of these include courses specifically focused on weddings. These four-year programs will give you the foundation of knowledge to begin your career in wedding planning. If you aren't in the position to study full-time, there are distance-learning classes and part-time programs available that may allow you to work and study at the same time.

Even after completing a degree program, you should be prepared to spend time gaining the hands-on experience that your school training just cannot provide. You may understand the process of developing an event, but you'll never be prepared for the unexpected curveballs that will be thrown at you on the job. Even with meticulous contingency planning, your ability to solve problems will often be tested at each wedding. Your book learning will certainly help with the planning back at the office, but only experience will give you the tools you need to plan and execute successful events on site.

My recommendation is to balance ongoing formal education with apprenticeships and strong mentors. Formal training will at least give you exposure on how to prepare for events. The danger lies in what you don't know. If you don't stay up on

Being the Best

Education:
- Formal training
- Monthly meetings offered by professional organizations
- Annual conferences

Experience:
- Networking with colleagues
- Apprenticeship with an experienced planner
- Ongoing self, peer, and client evaluations of your weddings and events

Don't overlook the importance of volunteering your time with a professional to get tips on best practices. Set time and money aside to take a course, attend a conference, or participate in a monthly industry meeting. Be critical of your planning procedures to create events that are safe and you are proud of.

risk procedures, you will not realize how dangerous some event situations can be. If you don't understand permitting, a surprise visit by the fire chief might shut down your tented affair while the guests are arriving. If you don't know the importance of involving the venue's engineering department when you are using fog machines, you may have the fire alarms blaring and the hotel evacuated an hour after the event begins. These are just a few details that if left unattended will result in event disaster. Training and experience will help you to be fully prepared for each event.

Professional Designations

There are many designations available in the hospitality industry. All are designed to meet the needs of training in different focal areas. If weddings and special events are your focus, the Certified Special Events Professional (CSEP) designation or the Professional Bridal Consultant (PBC) certification would also give you prestige and round out your skill set.

The format for the CSEP combines basic knowledge of the event-planning process with experience. This is a natural stepping-stone if you have completed classroom training and have worked for a few years, and now want to elevate your professional credentials.

The CSEP designation is offered by the International Special Events Society (ISES), and enrollment information can be found at www.ises.com. The process involves an application procedure with a submission of a point sheet calculating attendance and leadership in ISES, education, experience, industry and community service, and publications and awards. Once approved, you begin the preparation for the exam, which tests on core competencies in event management. The test is given in two parts: 100 multiple-choice questions and a written portion. The exam typically takes four hours or so to complete and is scored as a pass or fail.

Achieving certification or striving for a professional designation shows your ability to combine basic knowledge with implementation. It shows your commitment to professionalism in the industry. It will also set you apart from your competitors who are not certified.

Certified Professional Wedding Planner (CPWP): www.aa-wp.com
Certified Special Events Professional (CSEP): www.ises.com
Certified Wedding Planner (CWP): www.useventguide.com
Certified Wedding Specialist (CWS): www.weddingsbeautiful.com
Professional Bridal Consultant (PBC): www.bridalassn.com

The Association of Bridal Consultants offers both a professional and an accredited designation, giving you another opportunity to show your credentials not only to your clients but also to your vendors and colleagues. The accreditation process involves accruing membership points for education, experience, leadership and service, industry contributions, and related activities. Depending on the level of points you have, members can qualify for the Novice Consultant, Professional Bridal Consultant, Accredited Bridal Consultant, or Master Bridal Consultant designation. Applicants are required to submit a fee and complete two essays. To reach the Master Bridal Consultant level, you must also present a portfolio which is reviewed by a panel during the annual conference in November each year.

Check the sidebar for additional courses that offer designations and are available online.

Wedding vendors have the opportunity to become credentialed through the ABC as well as through many associations specific to their industry. It's a great idea to be aware of these designations to see which of your vendors are certified and are pros in their field. It helps to bring even more professionalism and value to your work, so don't be afraid to mention these successes to your prospects and clients.

Other Education Options

On-the-Job Training

While formal training provides a sound start for your business, on-the-job training will complement your book knowledge and provide the much-needed experience you need to become a "think-on-your-feet" professional. You might begin by working on projects with other experienced planners, or by volunteering in a community event that will utilize wedding-related services such as tenting, catering, or transportation. Be critical of the skills you have, and don't be afraid to step back from saying yes to a big project until you are ready. You will know when the time is right, but until then, reach out to others to build your skill set.

Ways to Gain Experience

Community events—fairs, parades, celebrations

Fund-raisers—"Save the Playground," "School Fun Fairs," "Walk for a Cure"

Venues—catering department, event department, summer outings

Vendors—assist linen company with setup, help planner with events, work with prop company or design firm with behind-the-scenes planning

Continuing Education Programs

If you are already working in the industry and want to round out your skills, check local listings for university, community college, or high school continuing education courses. Offerings can include courses in basic business skills, events skills, non-profit planning, catering, floral design, use of costuming or theatrical components in events, entertainment, public speaking, and marketing. These courses can be relatively inexpensive, are usually offered at convenient times and locations, and can provide an excellent base on which to build your business.

Industry Conferences and Courses

To really get an educational shot in the arm, commit to attending an industry conference. These conferences are great ways to receive training, network with fellow event professionals, and stay on top of current trends. They allow you to gather resources and ideas on how others execute the event process.

The Association of Bridal Consultants (www.bridalassn.com) holds an annual conference for its members each November, with a celebrity keynote speaker, education sessions, roundtables, a trade show, and off-site events. It's a great way to meet with other professionals, share challenges and ideas, and renew your creative energy for upcoming weddings. You can earn points for attendance that can be applied toward receiving your credentials (www.ises.com).

The International Special Events Society traditionally holds a three-day conference each August called Eventworld. The days are jam-packed with sessions on an array of event topics, and evenings typically allow the host city to showcase their best venues, decked out in contemporary, unique themes. At the ISES Esprit Awards Dinner, held on the final evening, prestigious industry awards are given to winners throughout the world. These conferences also provide ample time to network with fellow planners and chat about the event industry. The educational sessions also include a CSEP track with specific courses to help candidates prepare for certification. Attendance at these conferences will also help you to accrue points for certification. While more costly than local seminars and conferences, they will give you a very broad perspective of the industry and allow you to network with other planners from across the globe that may share your same challenges, but are not direct competitors.

The Special Event (TSE, www.thespecialeventshow.com) is held each January and delivers a similar experience. This conference has an additional trade-show feature with exhibitors showcasing products and services specifically used in the event industry. It is a great way to pick up new ideas to add pizzazz to your weddings. Daily educational sessions, evening parties, and a closing gala celebration awards dinner are also offered.

Event Solutions Expo (www.event-solutions.com) is held during late summer and offers a similar conference experience, combining education and a trade show.

The Professional Wedding Planners Conference of Canada (www.weddingplan nersconf.com) organizes several conferences and seminars throughout the year, with guest speakers, information on catering and marketing, and tips for planning multicultural weddings.

Seminars

The ABC features a variety of New Horizon Seminars which are held throughout the United States for anyone, from novice to pro. These are great ways to meet other professionals, get training, and learn about the basics of wedding planning.

Fred Pryor Seminars (www.pryor.com) offers a one-day workshop for those just starting out in event planning. The seminar features tips on successful wedding planning, including coordination of wedding details, communication issues, choosing the right team, creating a project plan, and controlling the big day. These workshops are offered both in the United States and Canada.

Regional Educational Conferences

You can also attend the regional educational conferences offered by both ISES and ABC, an option that may be closer to home and less expensive than the international conferences. The ABC regional conference is held in an area that is not hosting the annual conference and targets trends in the wedding business. The ISES regional conferences are held throughout the world and are organized in various regions (Northeast, Southeast, West, Midwest, Asia Pacific, and EurAfrica). These local experiences are much like the international conferences, with a similar combination of education, evening activities, and networking. There are sometimes award presentations and exhibitor showcases as well. Attending one of these conferences is a more affordable way of gaining information, completing CSEP training classes, and networking with colleagues.

Trade Shows

Trade shows can help you update your supplier list and provide networking opportunities. Many of the industry Web sites will offer information on shows that focus on event-related products and services. BizBash, held each October, is specifically designed for the special events industry. Others, such as the Stationery Show, focus on a narrow aspect of the business, but can provide excellent, up-to-date resource information for your wedding clients. Bridal expos, while focusing on the bride as a client, can also give you ideas on trends and resources.

A few online resources for finding bridal expos include the Association for Wedding Professionals International (www.afwpi.com/shows/index.html) and Here Come the Brides: The Elegant Bridal Experience (www.herecomethebrides.net). Here Come the Brides is a bridal show held five times a year in Southern California, from June to November, and features some of the best vendors in the local area. Their Web site offers articles, vendor resource lists for brides, and information for exhibitors. The Best Wedding Sites (www.bestweddingsites.com/BridalShows) offers a database of bridal expos and event-planning expos in the United States, Canada, and the Philippines.

The Original Wedding Expo (www.originalweddingexpo.com) is a long-running New England bridal show. It features vendors from every discipline and usually spans two days. With six shows a year, each show will reach out to one thousand brides and four thousand visitors in total.

Mentors

If you look through your resource directory or card file, I'm sure you will find a list of names that you regard as professionals in the industry. These pros can be an excellent source of advice and training as you start and grow your business. As long as you are not perceived as direct competition, many people are flattered by an interest in their business practices and will welcome the opportunity to coach you. You will also see how others handle business duties like billing, training employees, and event execution.

Another great place to find mentors will be at your local ISES meetings. Most seasoned professionals will be happy to share advice and offer help to someone who's just starting out. You may even become a valuable resource to them when they are asked to take on a wedding that's too large or they have two bookings for the same weekend.

Don't discount the importance of a mentor to support your growth in running a home-based business. I have taken advice from other successful home-based entrepreneurs for tips on how to balance home and work, how to find good temporary help, and how to manage my business like a pro.

A Sampling of Top Wedding Associations

National Wedding Associations

Association of Bridal Consultants

Association of Certified Professional Wedding Consultants

Association of Wedding Professionals

Association for Wedding Professionals International

Bridal Association of America

National Association of Wedding Professionals

National Bridal Service

Wedding and Special Events Association

Regional Wedding Associations

Austin Wedding and Event Coordinators

Lake Arrowhead Wedding Association (California)

Central Valley Bridal Association (California)

Association of Wedding Professionals (Dallas)

Maui Wedding Association

Mississippi Bridal Association

Outer Banks Wedding Association (North Carolina)

Twin City Bridal Association (Minnesota)

Other Resources

Association of Wedding Gown Specialists

Bridal Retailers Association

Bridal Show Producers International

International Special Events Society

Wedding and Event Videographers Association

Wedding Photojournalist Association

Wedding & Portrait Photographers International

Apprenticeships

Before you begin the time-consuming and emotionally intense process of starting a business, consider serving time as an apprentice. There may be a seasoned planner out there who's looking for someone to handle some of the day-to-day tasks and would be willing to train you and bring you up through the ranks. A retirement-age planner with no plan for passing the business down might be willing to sell you his or her business when the time is right.

Above and Beyond

Building a business is a challenging and rewarding task. Once you have established yourself in the industry, you may find that you are overwhelmed by the amount of work that comes your way; you need more weekend time for yourself; or you have too much wedding paraphernalia in your tiny home office! The benefits of going from your kitchen coffeepot to your desk in three seconds flat aren't quite as attractive as being able to host guests in the spare room that has become your home office. While working out of the home offers many benefits— convenience, and saving time and money—you may decide that it's time to bring your business to a new level to better work your wedding magic. Let's consider the options.

Sharing the Wealth

If time has become your biggest challenge, perhaps sharing your workload with another professional would be an alternative. If you have been active in professional industry groups, you may have met someone who shares or complements your style and has the same level of professionalism that you have built for your business. You may decide to delegate any "day-of" clients to this associate. Perhaps the on-site staffing of your weddings can be handled by this colleague, leaving you to fit in the planning when your schedule allows.

Sharing duties on your wedding projects will mean tightening up communication between the two of you, as well as your clients. You will want to present a cohesive picture and let your brides and their families know who to expect on their wedding day. Many clients will develop a close bond with their planner, which can make it more difficult to continue the comfort level through the wedding day. If you bring your colleague on from the get-go and let your clients know you will be there for them, this could be a good way to stay active but cut down on the weekend or evening commitments you will have during high wedding season.

Taking on a Partner

If you truly have found a colleague that you are willing to share your growing business with, perhaps a formal partnership is in order. This will mean a legal commitment to creating a business partnership, which in turn will allow you to share the liabilities and financial rewards of your company, giving you more time or freedom. Consider the value your partner will bring to the business. Perhaps they will have expertise that you don't have. Maybe their list of past weddings includes a type of celebration that you just haven't focused on. Perhaps they also have a home-based business, and the joining of forces will allow the two of you to expand into a larger space. Evaluate how equitable the businesses are and consult with an attorney and your accountant to draw up a contract that works for both of you.

Adding Staff

As my business grew, it became crucial to have extra hands available on an ongoing basis to manage some of the details that were becoming impossible to handle in my busy work week. I started with two paid interns who worked several days a week. They were able to follow up with clients, place wedding orders for stationery and favors, organize notebooks, and do research for new ideas to bring to my wedding business. I hated to see the semester end, and really enjoyed the energy they brought to my office.

It was important to create space for them to work, which necessitated moving a few decorative pieces out of my office to make way for a large worktable and desk for another computer and some additional filing cabinets. I also updated my technology to be able to save documents on a shared network, so Amanda and Michele could access files. They were both impressive workers and brought creativity, energy, and a fresh perspective to my workday, and to my projects! Starting with interns on a part-time basis will allow you to test out potential employees before you make the leap to hiring a full-time staffer.

Moving Your Office Out of the Home

Luckily, I was able to gently expand my work space as I added staff to my business. An adjoining hallway held a large shelving system for my supplies and project notebooks. My new colleagues were fine with my two dogs and one cat and the occasional interruptions by my family. A recent renovation of my home provided space in my garage for wedding supplies and file storage, allowing me to move older files from my office to the garage, creating more work space for me. Having two new people in my office made me assess work rules and did necessitate taking my dogs to obedience class to keep them out of the office. From this experience, I can see that in time, a new space might feel like a fresh new lease on my work space, giving me more privacy and room as my business warrants it.

If you aren't in a place where you can reorganize or renovate to update your home office needs, you might reach a point where a move seems like the best alternative. Some of the benefits of having a space outside the home might include fewer interruptions, a more-professional environment for working and meeting with clients, and more space for storage or working on projects. The downside is cost, travel time, and a commitment to leasing the space for an extended period of time. Only you will know when the time is right, if ever, to move your business out of the home. In my area, there are older buildings and warehouses that are being renovated into loft spaces. While rustic, these offer a less-expensive alternative to a posh new office building. You may even gain valuable storage space or a common area to meet with clients and vendors.

Taking this leap will mean a commitment to maintaining or growing your business; you must keep the clients coming in to help you pay for your new fixed monthly expenses. It may also require purchasing new or additional equipment. You may also be adding staff and changing the relationship with your contract labor, making them full-time employees, which will mean changes in recordkeeping for your business. If the time is right and your home office and business is bulging at the seams, this may be the right move for you.

What's Next?

You may reach a point with your business where you are ready for a change—whether it means selling it, passing it on to a family member, or starting a new or related venture that sparks your interest. You may have experienced certain elements of the wedding planning business that you want to focus on, such as design and decor, or stationery and printed invitations. If you have managed your business well and have a strong financial and client base, you could be in a position to sell your company. If you have a talented assistant or family member who is ready to take the reins, this could be an opportunity to continue your income stream or to get a nice sum of money for the years you have spent building your reputation and business.

When you start your business, the option of selling it or leaving the industry may seem like light years away. Nonetheless, each step you take along your career path should lead you toward owning a wedding planning business that will ultimately be a financial success. Spend wisely, work hard, and follow your heart. You may never want to step back from the important role of making wedding dreams come true; or, another passion may tug at your heartstrings, urging you down a different path. There are no secrets or easy answers to making the right decisions for your business, both personally and professionally. It's simply a matter of having passion for what you do, the ability to look at yourself critically, and the desire to be the best you can be. Take it one step at a time, and be proud of how your desire for excellence turns your clients' wedding celebrations into occasions of great joy.

What It Costs

Rental of a two-day 6x6-foot booth at a bridal expo: $600 to $900

Online certificate program through the Wedding Planning Institute (can take up to 10 weeks to complete): $695 to $795

Two-day-seminar program through the Wedding Planning Institute (held in various locations with live instructor): $1,075

Three-credit classes through the Wedding Planning Institute: $375

Monthly meetings offered by professional organizations: $35 to $70

Annual one-day seminars offered by professional organizations: $150

Annual three-day seminars offered by professional organizations: $550 to $1,200

Adding an intern to the team: $0 to $15 per hour

Adding a full-time employee to your team: $500 per week and up

Frequently Asked Questions

1. *Should I only hire vendors who have certificates in their trade?*
   Having a designation or certification is a great way to demonstrate that you have completed a set of requirements that include safe execution of your craft; but not all disciplines will have them. It would be a plus to have accredited vendors working with you in areas like pyrotechnics, lighting, and catering, which demand knowledge of safety issues. In areas like photography or videography, while it may be a benefit to be certified, these professionals may be selected more on style and design skills than on their certification. When undecided about selecting an uncertified vendor, consider their recommendations and portfolios to help with your decision-making process.

2. *Are certificate programs worth the money they ask for?*
   That's like asking if it's worthwhile to get an education. I think certificate programs are worth the money. While hands-on experience is invaluable, you can also learn from written material or presentations by others. Getting a certificate proves to yourself and others that you have had the perseverance and fortitude to balance your time and energy to include a commitment to study and self-improvement!

3. *I graduated with a bachelor's degree in business administration. Should I still try to get a degree in event planning?*
   A BS in business will be essential for you in your daily business dealings. The special events industry, specifically weddings, will draw on additional skills not covered in basic business courses. If you don't want to go back to school, consider attending a conference, trade show, or expo, or joining an industry association to balance your business skills with the creativity needed for wedding planning.

4. *Are there internship programs for those of us who are middle-aged, trying to get into the profession?*
   I will often hire women or men who are looking for a career change or a chance to get back into the workforce, to work on special projects. Weddings require lots of extra hands for assembling favors, setting up the day

before, or helping with ceremony details while another team is working on reception activities. Just because you have taken a break from a formal job or are in a transition period doesn't mean you don't have the skills or energy needed to work in the special events industry.

Appendix A: Industry Associations and Educational Resources

National Associations

Association of Bridal Consultants (ABC)

56 Danbury Road, Suite 11
New Milford, CT 06776
Phone: (860) 355-7000
Fax: (860) 354-1404
www.bridalassn.com

- Commonly known as ABC; an association for those servicing the wedding industry
- Offers a monthly newsletter, business name search, brochure critique, insurance support, referrals and job placement assistance, education, certification
- Membership Categories: Novice: $185/year; Consultant: $265/year; Vendor: $195/year; Auxiliary: $170/year; Corporate: $550/year
- Local themed meetings every few months hosted by that are state coordinators
- Seminars include annual conferences, New Horizons (for those starting out), and Expanding Horizons (for experienced planners)

Association of Certified Professional Wedding Consultants

7791 Prestwick Circle
San Jose, California 95135
Phone: (408) 528-9000
Fax: (408) 528-9333
www.acpwc.com

- Chapters in Georgia, Washington, Colorado, Texas; multiple chapters in Florida and California
- Courses offered: The Business of Wedding Planning, Financial Matters, Client Relations, Wedding Planning and Coordinating, Ceremonies and Receptions, Vendor Selection, Etiquette and Protocol
- Three-Step Internship Program: Level I Certificate of Completion, Level II Professional Wedding Consultant, Level III Certified Wedding Consultant

Association for Wedding Professionals International

7791 Prestwick Circle
San Jose, California 95135
Phone: (408) 528-9000
Fax: (408) 528-9333
www.afwpi.com

- International association for those who service or plan weddings
- Web site is a member referral resource, giving information to those looking for planners or planners looking for other members
- Web site has links for both brides and professionals

Bridal Association of America

531 "H" Street
Bakersfield, CA 93304
Phone: (866) MY WEDDING
Fax: (661) 633-9199
www.bridalassociationofamerica.com

- Web site is designed to help brides plan their weddings
- Wedding professionals can sign up on the Web site to receive e-mail leads

International Special Events Society (ISES)

401 N. Michigan Avenue, Suite 2200
Chicago, IL 60611
Phone: (800) 688-4737
Fax: (312) 673-6953
www.ises.com

- Membership benefits include online service finder, promotions and discounts, and member magazine
- Forty local chapters with educational meetings held several times a year
- ISES Annual Meeting, Eventworld, held each summer
- Membership fees from $299 to $399 a year, special $35 student rate

National Association of Wedding Professionals

www.nawp.com

- Web site for wedding professionals and brides
- Articles on hiring help, bridal fashion, wedding expos
- Database of vendors by region

National Bridal Service

1004 West Thompson Street, Suite 205
Richmond, VA 23230
Phone: (804) 342-0055
Fax: (804) 342-6062
www.nationalbridal.com

- Web site with directory of bridal services, including rings, wedding gowns, and invitations
- Advertising for wedding professionals is available on Web site

Wedding and Special Events Association

2550 Pacific Coast Highway, Suite 213
Torrance, CA 90505
Phone: (310) 530-3003
www.wsea.com

- Web site designed to create a network of event-planning professionals
- Most of the advertised professionals are in the Torrance, California, area (310 area code)

Regional Wedding Associations

Association of Wedding Professionals
P.O. Box 743005
Dallas, TX 75374
www.awpdallas.com

- Group designed for Dallas and Fort Worth, Texas, wedding professionals
- Association provides educational programs, networking opportunities, and special event showcases
- Membership rates vary from $25 to $99

Austin Wedding and Event Coordinators
P.O. Box 28053
Austin, Texas 78755
Phone: (512) 860-AMOR
www.awec.org

- Web site for Austin, Texas, couples looking for event professionals in the area
- Membership fees are $45 to $75 per year, $20 fee per meeting
- Information for coordinators on getting started, acquiring business, and being a consultant

Boston Wedding Group (BWG)
Phone: (978) 210-2136
www.bostonweddinggroup.com

- Composed of nearly sixty wedding professionals in the Boston area
- Members must complete application to gain acceptance
- Companies span a great many disciplines, from cakes to formal wear to photographers

Central Valley Bridal Association
www.centralvalleybridal.com

- A comprehensive site of resources and vendors located in the Fresno, California, area

- Provides marketing and advertising for wedding professionals in the area

Lake Arrowhead Wedding Association

P.O. Box 618
Lake Arrowhead, CA 92352
Phone: (909) 337-8849
www.lakearrowheadweddings.com

- Web site for Lake Arrowhead–area couples looking for wedding professionals in the area
- Site also provides information for those planning a destination wedding or honeymoon to Lake Arrowhead

The Maui Wedding Association

www.mauiweddingassociation.com

- Offers resources for planners or couples planning a wedding in Hawaii
- Provides valuable information for destination planners
- Articles and resources on planning weddings in Hawaii
- Offers honeymoons such as top ten beaches, restaurants, sightseeing

Mississippi Bridal Association

P.O. Box 6601
Jackson, MS 39282
Phone: (601) 988-1142
Fax: (601) 988-1142
www.msbridalassoc.com

- Full listing of Mississippi wedding professionals
- Brides and industry professionals can join the site
- Holds a yearly Mississippi Bridal Show

Outer Banks Wedding Association (OBWA)

P.O. Box 1067
Kill Devil Hills, NC 27948
www.outerbanksweddingassoc.org

- 200 members on database, a good resource for destination weddings in the North Carolina Outer Banks area
- Web site earns 1,000 bridal leads yearly

Twin City Bridal Association (TCBA)
4050 Olson Memorial Highway, Suite 170
Minneapolis, Minnesota 55422
Phone: (763) 529-1900
Fax: (763) 529-1922
www.twincitybridal.com

- Resource-filled site for those in the Twin City area, with a comprehensive list of vendors and educational opportunities
- Web site features free literature for engaged couples
- TCBA puts on an annual wedding fair with a large showing of industry professionals

Certificate Programs

Professional Planning Designations:

- Certified Professional Wedding Planner (CPWP)—www.aa-wp.com
- Certified Special Event Professional (CSEP)—www.ises.org
- Certified Wedding Professional (CWP)—www.useventguide.com
- Certified Wedding Specialist (CWS)—www.weddingsbeautiful.com
- Professional Bridal Consultant (PBC)—www.bridalassn.com

Vendor Designations:
Catering
National Association of Catering Executives (NACE), www.nace.net
NACE offers certification in catering, the Certified Professional Catering Executive (CPCE).

Photography
Professional Photographers of America (PPA), www.ppa.com

A photographer with certification gets the title of Certified Professional Photographer (CPP).

Videography
Wedding and Event Videography Association (WEVA), www.weva.com
WEVA has an accredited program in which graduates earn the Merited Professional Videographer (MPV).

Rentals
American Rental Association (ARA), www.ararental.org
ARA has a Certified Event Rental Professional (CERP) designation gained through completing an educational program.

Tents
Industrial Fabrics Association International (IFAI), www.ifai.com
IFAI offers several professional designations for those in the tent industry, including the Certified Project Planner (CPP).

Wedding Certificate Programs

American Academy of Wedding Professionals (AAWP)
www.aa-wp.com
The International School of Hospitality (TISOH)
www.tisoh.com/programs_wedding.html
Penn Foster Career School
www.pennfoster.edu/bridalconsultant/index.html?semkey=Q088528
Wedding Coordination and Design Certificate Program, The Wedding Planning Institute (WPI)
www.weddingplanninginstitute.com

Additional Industry Conferences and Courses

Engage!08, www.engage08.com
A one-day, high-impact wedding business symposium.

The Wedding Planners Institute of Canada, www.weddingplanners conf.com
This organization puts on several conferences and seminars throughout the year with guest speakers, information on catering and marketing, and tips for planning multicultural weddings.

Two-Day Certification Seminar, (877) 597-8166, www.weddingplanning institute.com/wedding_planning_seminar_details_sonoma.html
Fairmont Sonoma Mission Inn & Spa Destination Resort
100 Boyes Boulevard
Sonoma, CA 95476
A classroom-style seminar taught by professionals.

College and University Programs

Online Courses: Wedding Planning Certification
Chesapeake College: 8-week class; Contact Elaine Wilson, (410) 827-5835
www.chesapeake.edu/continuing_ed/ce_sched.asp
Economic Development Center Building, Room: EDC-27
P.O. Box 8
Wye Mills, MD 21679

Kishwaukee Community College: 10-week class; Contact Continuing Education Program Director, stefani@kishwaukeecollege.edu, (815) 825-2086, www.kishwaukee college.edu
21193 Malta Road
Malta, IL 60150

Macomb Community College: Contact Valerie Corbett CPP, Program Coordinator, Center for Continuing Education, (586) 498-4002, corbettv@macomb.edu, www .macomb.edu
14500 E. 12 Mile Road
Warren, MI 48088

Manatee Community College: Contact Office of Continuing Education, (888) 221-9988 x.903, admissions@wpi-edu.com

Southeast Community College: Contact Continuing Education, (402) 437-2700 or 1-800-828-0072, nholman@southeast.edu, www.southeast.edu
301 S. 68th Street Place
Lincoln, Nebraska 68510

College/University Classroom Class: Wedding Planning Certification

Austin Community College: 8-week class; Contact Addie Kellington, (512) 223-7813, akelling@austincc.edu, www.austincc.edu/ce/cp/wedding
Highland Business Center
5930 Middle Fiskville Road
Austin, TX 78752

Carroll Community College: 10-week class; Contact Office of Continuing Education, (410) 386-8100, cet@carrollcc.edu, www.carrollcc.edu
1601 Washington Road
Westminster, MD 21157

Clark College: 10-week class; Contact Sarah, Program Developer, Office of Corporate & Continuing Education, (360) 992-2939, http://at-campus.net/clark/category/category.aspxT-Building
1933 Fort Vancouver Way MS TBG237
Vancouver, WA 98663

Delaware Tech. Community College: Stanton Campus Wedding Planning Certification; 10-week class; Contact Kathy Linsner, Office of Continuing Education, (302) 453-3072, klinsner@dtcc.edu, www.dtcc.edu/ccpsw/business_courses.html#eyd645
400 Stanton-Christiana Road, Office A-165
Newark, DE 19713

Edison College: 10-week class; Contact Lisa Dick, Office of Continuing Education, ldick@edison.edu, http://edison.edu/lee/ce/business/Wedding%20Planner%20Certification.pdf

Lee Campus
8099 College Parkway
Fort Myers, FL 33919

Elgin Community College: 10-week class; Contact Donna Newberg, Program Developer, Continuing Education, (847) 214-7569, dnewberg@elgin.edu, www.elgin.edu/noncreditclasses.aspx?Category=WEDNG
1700 Spartan Drive
Elgin, IL 60123

Erie Community College: 8-week class; Contact Carrie Kahn, Continuing Education Office, (716) 270-5167, kahn@ecc.edu, www.ecc.edu/paths/noncredit.asp
4041 Southwestern Blvd.
Orchard Park, NY 14127

Glendale Community College: 10-week class; Contact General Registration, Office of Continuing Education, (818) 240-1000 Ext 5015, www.glendale.edu/cse
Toll Middle School
700 Glenwood Road
Glendale, CA 91202

Miami Dade—Kendall: 10-week class; Contact Irene Baquero, Office of Continuing Education, (305) 237-2747, ibaquero@mdc.edu, www.mdc.edu/kendall/ce/MDC
Kendall Campus
11011 SW 104 Street
Miami, FL 33176-3393

Miami Dade—Miami Lakes: 10-week class; Contact Marlin Alba, Office of Continuing Education, (305) 237-1303, malba@mdc.edu, www.mdc.edu/ce/north
Barbara Goleman Sr. High School, Miami Lakes, FL

Miami Dade—West Campus: 10-week class; Contact Evette, Office of Continuing Education, (305) 237-8914, www.mdc.edu/ce
MDC West Campus, Doral, FL

Miami Dade—Wolfson: 10-week class; Contact Ada Pernas, Office of Continuing Education, (305) 237-3821, apernas@mdc.edu, www.communityeducationatwolfson.com/MDC
Wolfson Campus
300 NE 2nd Ave, Room 1158
Miami, FL 33132

St. Petersburg College: Contact Jackie Addis, Program Director, Lifelong Learning Department, (727) 341-3184, Addis.Jackie@spcollege.edu, Clearwater, FL

Tennessee State University: 10-week class; Contact Cheryl Kurowski, (877) 597-8166, ckurowski@lovegevity.com
Avon Williams Campus, Nashville, TN

The University of Akron: Contact Workforce Development, Continuing Education, (330) 972-7577, www.uakron.edu/ce, Buckingham 56, Akron, OH

University of New Mexico: 10-week class; Contact Marie McGhee, Office of Continuing Education, (505) 277-0723
1634 University Blvd. N.E.
Albuquerque, NM 87102

University of Richmond: 10-week class; Contact Holly Howze, Program Developer, Continuing Education, (804) 289-8133, hhowze@richmond.edu, www.richmond.edu
Jepson Hall, Room 108
28 Westhampton Way
Richmond, VA 23173

University of Texas–Arlington: 10-week class; Contact Cassandra Smith, Program Developer, Continuing Education, (817) 272-3713, casssm@uta.edu, www.uta.edu/ced, http://weddingplanningcertificationuniversityoftexas.scribestudio.com/custom/9344/index.jsp?
140 Mitchell
Arlington, Texas 76019

Wagner College: 10-week class; Contact Sharon P. Guinta, Program Developer, Continuing Education, (718) 390-3221, sharon.guinta@wagner.edu, www.wagner.edu
External Programs/One Campus Road
Staten Island, NY 10301

Allied Associations

American Disc Jockey Association (ADJA), www.adja.org

American Rental Association (ARA), www.ararental.org
1900 19th Street
Moline, IL 61265
Phone: (800) 334-2177
Fax: (309) 764-1533

- ARA offers the resources needed for success in the rental market
- Offers member benefits including connection to industry people and information on products, services, and information

Association of Wedding Gown Specialists, www.weddinggownspecialists.com
Phone: (800) 501-5005

- Features valuable information on cleaning, restoration, and preservation of wedding gowns
- Wedding Gown Specialists are recommended by bridal designers, museums, and popular magazines

Bridal Show Producers International (BSPI), www.bspishows.com
4957 SE Lakemont Boulevard SE, C1-04
Bellevue, WA 98006
Phone: (425) 922-7924

- Complete listing of all international and national bridal shows
- Web site accessible to show producers, wedding industry professionals, and brides
- Can be a member for an annual fee of $595

Industrial Fabrics Association International (IFAI), www.ifai.com
1801 County Road B W

Roseville, MN 55113
Phone: (800) 225-4324

- IFAI is the trade association representing the specialty fabric industry
- Members are offered referrals, business discounts, and networking opportunities

International Caterers Association, www.icacater.org
91 Timberlane Drive
Williamsville, NY 14221
Phone: (877) 422-4221
Fax: (888) 210-4634

- ICA is an association that provides education for caterers, chefs, students, event planners, and other vendors

National Association of Catering Executives (NACE), www.nace.net
9881 Broken Land Parkway, Suite 101
Columbia, MD 21046
Phone: (410) 290-5410
Fax: (410) 290-5460

- Offers networking opportunities, professional certification, education programs, and a job bank
- State and regional chapters offer informative network meetings throughout the year

National Wedding Retailers Association (NWRA), www.aboutnwra.com
1150 Ninth Street, Suite 1400
Modesto, CA 95354
Phone: (866) 292-6972

- Focus on wedding attire specialists
- Provides retailers with training in business education programs

Professional Photographers of America (PPA), www.ppa.com
229 Peachtree St. NE, Suite 2200
Atlanta, GA 30303

Phone: (800) 786-6277

Fax: (404) 614-6400

- An industry association for photographers offering business protection, education, and professional recognition
- Offers certification for photographers

Wedding and Event Videography Association (WEVA), www.weva.com

Tamiami Trail, PMB 208

Sarasota, FL 34238

Phone: (941) 923-5334

Fax: (941) 921-3836

- Trade association for videographers to network and gain business leads
- Membership fee is about $185 a year
- Web site features industry news, forums for discussion, and a "Brides' Guide"

Wedding Photojournalist Association (WPJA), www.wpja.com

- Couples can find photographers from the large database that includes international professionals
- Includes articles from *Wedding Photography Magazine*
- Membership opportunity for photographers

Wedding & Portrait Photographers International (WPPI), www.wppionline.com

6059 Bristol Parkway, Suite 100

Culver City, CA 90230

Phone: (310) 846-4940

Fax: (310) 846-5995

- Web site has photographer database, competitions, and a newsletter
- Membership is about $99 a year
- Offers educational programs and a heavily attended annual convention

Appendix B: Wedding Planning Resources

Suggested Reading by Chapter

Chapter 1: Saying "I Do" to Becoming a Wedding Planner!
Bridal Market Advertising Guide, National Mail Order Association, www.nmoa
.org/catalog/bridalguide.htm
Brides Magazine, www.brides.com
Consumerism, Romance, and the Wedding Experience by Sharon Boden
Modern Bride, www.modernbride.com
www.bibliomaven.com/businessjournals.html
www.bibliomaven.com/citymags.htm
www.bizjournals.com

Chapter 2: Working Out of the Home:
The Home Office Book by Donna Paul, Grey Crawford
Organizing Your Home Office for Success: Expert Strategies that Can Work for You by Lisa Kanarek

Chapter 3: The Balancing Act
High-Wire Mom: Balancing Your Family and a Business at Home by Kendra Smiley
The Work at Home Balancing Act: The Professional Resource Guide for Managing Yourself, Your Work, and Your Family at Home by Sandy Anderson

Chapter 4: Developing Your Business
Business Planning Web sites:
www.AllBridalStores.com

www.AllWeddingCompanies.com
www.BridalBuyersGuide.com
www.BridalFashionMall.com
www.bridalshowexpo.com
www.BridalTips.com
www.DiscountBridalService.com
www.1800bride2B.com
www.TheKnot.com
www.modernbride.com
www.nationalbridal.com/index
www.RespondWeddings.com
www.sellthebride.com
www.WeddingChannel.com

Chapter 5: Dollars and Sense

Home Business Tax Deductions: Keep What You Earn by Stephen Fishman and Diana Fitzpatrick

QuickBooks 2007 for Dummies by Stephen L. Nelson

Chapter 6: Marketing Your Services

How to Market Your Business: A Practical Guide to Advertising, PR, Selling, and Direct and Online Marketing by Dave Patten

Small Business Marketing for Dummies (2nd Ed.) by Barbara Findlay Schenck

Chapter 7: Running Your Business

Developing Teams through Project-Based Learning by Jean Atkinson

Small Business: Developing the Winning Management Team by George W. Rimler

Team Building: Proven Strategies for Improving Team Performance by William G. Dyer, W. Gibb Dyer Jr., Jeffrey H. Dyer, and Edgar H. Schein

Chapter 8: Legal Matters

Complete Idiot's Guide to Law for Small Business Owners by Stephen Maple

Legal Forms for Starting & Running a Small Business by Fred S. Steingold

Legal Guide for Starting & Running A Small Business (8th Ed.) by Fred S. Steingold and Ilona M. Bray

www.elmsoftware.com (iDo Wedding and Event Professional Edition)
www.entrepreneur.com (Web site for business owners)
www.kiplinger.com (Small Business Center)
www.legalzoom.com (Online Legal Document Services)
www.sba.gov (Small Business Administration)
www.smallbusinessreview.com (resources for small business owners)

Chapter 9: Wedding Planning Basics

The Complete Book of Wedding Crafts by Rockport Publishers
Gala!: The Special Event Planner for Professionals and Volunteers by Patti Coons
I Do: A Guide to Creating Your Own Unique Wedding Ceremony by Sydney Barbara Metrick
The Knot Book of Wedding Flowers by Carley Roney
Weddings by Colin Cowie
Weddings, Dating, and Love Customs of Cultures Worldwide, Including Royalty by Carolyn Mordecai

Chapter 10: Unique Wedding Trends: The Old and the New

Green products

Green Home: The Environmental Store

www.greenhome.com, Phone: (415) 282-6400

National Geographic's Green Guide Product List

www.thegreenguide.com/products

Green event-planning resources

www.californiaorganicflowers.com
www.ecochicweddings.com
www.eco-limo.com
www.ecospeakers.com/foreventmgrs/greenevents/index.html
www.evolimo.com
www.islandbrides.com/view-article/Green+Weddings/48
www.lights4fun.co.uk/
www.macys.com
www.nativeenergy.com/portovert
www.oblationpapers.com

www.organicbouquet.com
www.ozocar.com
www.pancakeandfranks.com
www.3rliving.com

Destination support services

Beach Weddings and Destination Weddings in the Caribbean, www.islandbrides.com

Beverly Clark's WeddingLocation.com, www.weddinglocation.com

Destination Bride, www.destinationbride.com

DestinationWeddings.com, www.destinationweddings.com

Destination Weddings and Honeymoons, www.destinationweddingmag.com
Phone: (407) 628-4802

Destination Weddings by The Knot, www.destinationweddingsbytheknot.com
Phone: (877) THE KNOT, *The Knot Guide to Destination Weddings* by Carley Roney
with Joann Gregoli

The Travel Institute, www.thetravelinstitute.com

The Wedding Experience: Weddings around the World, Phone: (877) 580-3556,
www.theweddingexperience.com

Wedding Regulations around the World, www.lovetripper.com/article/wedding-regulations/index.html

Cultural resources

www.theknot.com/keywords/sc_161_527.shtml
www.weddingsolutions.com/article/Wedding_Cultural_Traditions_1.html
www.wedthemes.com/cultural-weddings.shtml

Same-sex weddings

GayWeddings.com, www.gayweddings.com
Phone: (866) 900-3164

IDoInToronto.com, www.idointoronto.com
Phone: (888) 418-1188

The Knot Same-Sex Weddings, www.theknot.com/keywords/in_198.shtml

Charity

Changing the Present, www.changingthepresent.org/weddings

I Do Foundation, www.idofoundation.org
Phone: (866) 587- 8448

JustGive, www.justgive.org/weddings/index.jsp

Recycle Your Wedding, www.recycleyourwedding.com

World Wildlife Fund, www.worldwildlife.org/weddings

Other resources for your wedding planning skill set

Becoming a Carlson Craft Dealer, www.carlsoncraft.com
Phone: (800) 580-1707

Becoming an Ordained Minister, www.ordination.com
Phone: (559) 297-4271

Butterfly Release Course, www.forbutterflies.org

Learning Calligraphy, www.calligraphycentre.com

Learning to Sew, www.patternreview.com

List of Floral Design Schools, www.800florals.com/care/designSchools.asp

Chapter 11: E-Commerce and Internet Use

Business support

Book More Weddings: More Brides, More Inquiries, More Sales, www.bookmoreweddings.com

Business Data and Statistics, www.firstgov.gov/Business/Business_Data.shtml

Custom Web site Design, www.godaddy.com

eMarketer, www.emarketer.com

Fastest Way to Write a Business Plan, www.paloalto.com

Free Economic, Demographic & Financial Data, www.economy.com/freelunch/default.asp

How to Help Your Wedding or Invitation Business Grow, www.sellthebride.com

Internet Retailer, www.Internetretailer.com

NJWedding.com Business Resource Center for New Jersey, New York, and Pennsylvania Wedding Professionals, www.njwedding.com/business

State Information, www.firstgov.gov/Agencies/State_and_Territories.shtml

U.S. Small Business Administration, www.sba.gov

WeddingIndustry.biz: Business Resource Center, www.weddingindustry.biz

Resources for ceremonies

http://catholicsensibility.wordpress.com

www.aish.com/literacy/lifecycle/Guide_to_the_Jewish_Wedding.asp

www.altweddings.com

www.bestdestinationwedding.com/forum

www.catholicbrides.com

www.gayweddings.com

www.gayweddingsoncapecod.com

www.gayweddingworld.com

www.glad.org/marriage/howtogetmarried.html

www.kingdomquest.com/weddings.html

www.loc.gov/rr/business/wedding/wedding.html

www.myqueerwedding.com

www.ourweddingsongs.com

www.outvite.com

www.theweddingreport.com

www.topweddingsites.com/wedding-music.html

www.twogrooms.com

www.wedalert.com/songs

www.weddingvendors.com/music

Chapter 12: Being the Best

Exceptional Events: Concept to Completion (2nd Ed.), by Elizabeth A. Wiersma, CSEP, and Kari E. Strolberg

Introduction to Hospitality by John R. Walker

Special Events: Best Practice in Modern Event Management (2nd Ed.), by Dr. Joe Jeff Goldblatt, CSEP

Index

A

ABC. *See* Association of Bridal Consultants (ABC)
accountants, 59, 60
advertising, 90, 97, 182, 183
African wedding customs, 161
AFWPI (Association for Wedding Professionals International), 193
agencies, trained staff, 110–11
alcohol permits, 125
apprenticeships, 186, 195
Armenian wedding customs, 161
assistants. *See* staffing support
Association for Wedding Professionals International (AFWPI), 193
Association of Bridal Consultants (ABC)
    membership benefits, 28, 41, 91
    training opportunities, 6, 191, 192
Association of Wedding Professionals, 91
associations, professional
    conferences, 191–92
    lists of, 194
    membership benefits, 51, 91
    membership costs, 113
    networking opportunities through, 28, 41–42
    as staffing source, 110
    as trade show sponsors, 192–93
attorneys, 30, 59, 60, 83, 118–19

B

babysitters, 36–38, 39, 171
balance sheets, 56
BizBash, 192
bookkeepers, 59
Bridal Association of America, 11
bridal fairs, 90
brochures, 87
budgets
    for business planning, 64–66, 78
    for wedding planning, 73–75, 132, 152, 155

business cards, 60–61, 82, 87, 97
business costs
    home office set up, 24
    Internet usage, 182
    liability and legal advice, 130
    marketing, 96
    planning details, 154
    professional association memberships, 113
    professional service fees, 59, 130
    schedule planning and balance, 37
    of staffing support, 113
    start-up expenses, 64
business development
    balance sheets, 56
    cash-flow analyses, 56–57
    company structure decisions, 42–45
    credentials, biography and résumé, 51–53
    expansion, 195–97
    financial plan, 55–56
    identity creation, 48–49, 81–82
    income statement, 56
    marketing plans, 54
    market research, 45–48
    mission statement, 49
    networking for, 41–42
    objectives, 50–51
    operations plan, 55
    organizational charts, 53–54
    short- and long-term goals, 57–60
    special status with state agencies, 177–78

C

career day presentations, 95
cash-flow analyses, 56
cash-flow statements and projections, 66–67, 68
Catholic weddings, 160
ceremonies
    checklists for, 149
    cultural customs, 161–63

general costs, 174
    procession order, traditional, 159
    religious, 160–61
    traditional elements of, 158–59, 175
certificate programs, 187–88, 199
charity contributions, 173, 181
checklists, wedding, 149–50
child care, 36–38, 39, 171
Chinese wedding customs, 162
client binders, 22–23, 134, 140–41
clients
    agreements and contracts, 118–19, 121–24
    assessing personalities for wedding styles, 157–58
    first year business goals, 29
    initial conversations and meetings with, 132–33, 135–37
    marketing plans, 5
    negotiating fees with, 71–72
    organizing information on, 22–23, 134, 140–41
    recap meetings and evaluation feedback, 154
    selection of, 15
    testimonials from, 83
company names, 48–49, 82–83, 184
competition, 46
computer technology, 21–22
conduct, professional, 128–29
conferences, 191–92
contracts, 118–24, 130, 134
copyright issues, 125
creativity credit, 129
credentials, 51–53. See also training and education
cuisine, 152
cultural customs, 161–63

D
DBA (Doing Business As), 42, 43
decorations, 152
defining statements, 81–82
deposits, 63
designations, professional, 187–89, 190
destination weddings, 164–72, 175
Doing Business As (DBA), 42, 43
Dutch wedding customs, 162

E
e-commerce. See Internet; Web sites
education. See training and education
"elevator speeches," 81–82

employees, permanent, 114, 125, 131, 196–97, 198. See also staffing support
entertainment, 152
ethics, event, 128–29
evaluations, 112, 154
events, additional, 149, 170, 175
Event Solutions Expo, 191
experience, 14, 51–52, 189–90, 195. See also training and education
expos, bridal, 193, 198

F
family balance. See schedule planning and balance
finances
    bank account management, 72–73
    budget development for business, 64–66, 78
    budgeting for individual weddings, 73–75
    cash-flow statements, 66–67
    income taxes, 75
    investment spending, 63
    invoice samples, 76–77
    management tools for, 56–57
    off-season services, 57
    online management of, 177
    pricing and fees (see pricing and fees)
financial vocabulary, 63
fire prevention and safety, 153, 156
Fred Pryor Seminars, 192
French wedding customs, 162

G
Gay & Lesbian Advocates & Defenders, 174
gay/lesbian weddings, 174
German wedding customs, 162
gifts, vs. charity contributions, 173–74
goal setting, 57–60
graphic designers, 59
Greek wedding customs, 162
green weddings, 172–73, 176
guest lists, 151, 173

H
Here Come the Brides (bridal expo), 193
home offices. See also schedule planning and balance
    business supplies, 22
    client information organization, 22–23
    environment, 26–27

equipment for, 20
marketing materials, 23
organization of, 27–28
outside-home spaces vs., 197
overview of basic needs, 23
resources, samples and supplies, 24–26
set up costs, 24
software needs, 21–22, 27, 154
specialty planning tools, 23
technological needs, 21
work space selection and design, 19–20
honeymoons, 87, 173
hotels, 93

I

identity, business, 48–49, 81–82
income statements, 56
incorporating, 44
Indian wedding customs, 162
insurance, 125–26, 130, 131
International Professional Special Events Society, 128
International Special Events Society (ISES)
 membership benefits, 28, 42, 91
 training opportunities, 6, 191, 192
Internet. *See also* Web sites
 bridal expo information, 193
 charity contributions, 181
 finance management online, 177
 general costs of, 182
 scam warnings, 130–31
 special status research online, 177–78
 supplier contacts, 181
 wedding trend research, 182
interns and internships, 109, 196, 198, 199–200
iPhones, 21, 90
Irish wedding customs, 162
ISES. *See* International Special Events Society (ISES)
Italian wedding customs, 162

J

Japanese wedding customs, 162
Jewish weddings, 161

K

Korean wedding customs, 162

L

letterhead and stationery, 84, 87, 97
liability
 business structure choices and, 42–45
 contracts, 118–24, 130, 134
 event ethics, 128–29
 general costs, 130
 insurance, 125–26, 130
 overview of, 115–16
 permits and licenses, 124–25
 risk assessments and plans, 126–28
 troubleshooting tips on, 116–17
licenses
 marriage, 158
 miscellaneous requirements for weddings, 124–25, 155, 171
limited liability companies (LLCs), 43, 44–45
listening skills, 134
location selection, 151. *See also* destination weddings
logos, 82, 83, 84, 98

M

magazines
 bridal, 182
 writing articles for, 95, 97
marketing. *See also* networking
 communication skills for, 5, 8
 creating an identity, 48–49, 81–82
 creating plans and opportunities for, 54, 88–96
 first impressions, 89
 general costs, 96
 information research and plan for, 45–47
 materials for, 23, 81–86, 87, 97
 phases for, 86
 promotional tools, 87–88
 self-assessments for, 80–81
 techniques for, 57
marriage licenses, 158
MBDA (Minority Business Development Agency), 178
mentors, 186, 193
Mexican wedding customs, 162
Microsoft FrontPage, 22
Minority Business Development Agency (MBDA), 178
minority-owned businesses, 177–78
mission statements, 50
music, 125, 152, 158–59

N

networking
    for clients, 15, 39, 83
    overview, 92–94
    for small business advice, 41–42
    for vendors, 28, 106–8
New Horizon seminars, 192
newspapers, writing articles for, 95, 97

O

objectives, business, 50–51
Office of Small and Disadvantaged Business
    Utilization (OSDBU), 178
operations plans, 55
optimism vs. reality, 14–15
Original Wedding Expo, 193
OSDBU (Office of Small and Disadvantaged
    Business Utilization), 178
outdoor weddings, 152–53, 155–56

P

partnerships, 43–44, 196
payment policies, 117, 119, 121, 170, 179
PayPal, 179
permits, 124–25, 152–53, 155, 171
personal digital assistant (PDA), 21
Polish wedding customs, 163
portfolios, 88
postcards, 87, 88
PowerPoint, 21, 87
pricing and fees
    ethics and, 128–29
    first client meetings and discussion of, 133
    negotiations, 66, 71–72, 153
    recordkeeping, 15, 137
    specialized events and activities, 175
    structuring and choices, 67, 69–71
printers, 21
procession order, traditional, 159
Professional Wedding Planners Conference of
    Canada, 192
proposals, 23, 134
Protestant weddings, 160–61

Q

questionnaires, wedding, 135–36
QuickBooks, 21

R

receptions, 150, 151, 152, 159–60
religious weddings, 160–61
rentals, 152
reputation, 128–29
résumés, 51–53
rice tossing, 159

S

same-sex weddings, 174, 175
schedule planning and balance
    child care, 36–38, 39
    community volunteering, 36
    costs, 37
    family time, 33–34
    personal time, 34–35, 40
    prioritizing, 30–31
    setting parameters, 38–39
    socializing, 35, 40
    support systems, 39
    weekly to-do list samples, 32–33
    work time, 31–32, 40
SCORE (Service Corps of Retired Executives), 42,
    78
Scottish wedding customs, 163
self-assessments
    financial planning, 4–5
    job descriptions and considerations, 13–16
    job responsibilities, 2
    marketing and, 80–81
    personality requirements, 2–4
    and self-commitment, 16
    skill requirements, 4, 10
    strength and weaknesses, 11–13, 47
    timing and dedication, 4, 9, 12, 13
    training and experience, 5, 6–8, 12, 17, 18
selling the business, 197–98
seminars, 192, 198
Service Corps of Retired Executives (SCORE), 42,
    78
skills
    business, overview, 7, 13, 14, 100, 102
    communication, 5, 7–8, 163
    listening, 134
    requirements, 99–105
software, computer, 21–22, 27, 154
sole proprietor, 42–43
speaking engagements, 95–96
Special Event, The, 191
specialization
    cultural customs, 161–63

destination weddings, 164–72, 175
  generalization vs., 61
  overview, 10
  religious weddings, 160–61
  same-sex weddings, 174, 175
  tented/outdoor weddings, 152–53, 155–56
staffing support. *See also* vendors
  communicating expectations, 8
  costs, 113
  determining needs, 113, 153
  duties of, 108
  insurance for, 131
  permanent employees, 114
  sources for, 109–11
  volunteers, 114
statements
  defining/branding, 81–82
  marketing, 85
  mission, 50
State Office of Minority and Women Business
  Assistance (SOMWBA), 177–78
stationery, 84, 87, 97
suppliers, 181
Swedish wedding customs, 163

T
taxes, income, 75
tax identification numbers, 43
tented weddings, 152–53, 155–56
testimonials, 83
theme and concept development, 150–51
time line plans, 137–40, 146, 164–69
time management, 14
toolboxes, on-site wedding, 25, 26
trade shows, 90, 192–93
traditional weddings, 158–59, 175
training and education
  apprenticeships, 195
  continuing education programs, 101, 190–91
  formal education, 185–89, 199
  general costs, 198
  industry conferences, courses and seminars,
    191–92
  job requirements, 6–8
  mentors, 193
  as networking opportunities, 94–95
  on-the-job, 14, 189–90
  trade shows, 192–93
  volunteering for, 15
transportation, 170–71
Turkish wedding customs, 163

U
U.S. Small Business Administration, 41, 78

V
vendor lists, preferred, 97
vendors
  communicating with, 8
  contracts and, 119, 120
  creating contacts, 28, 105–6
  criteria for, 107
  ethics and, 131
  hotels as, 93
  information researching on, 111
  job evaluations, 112
  job requirements and expectations, 112
  negotiating prices with, 72
  networking for clients, 94
  operations plan and, 55
  organizational worksheets, 142–45
  out of town, for destination weddings, 113–14
  professional designations/certifications for,
    189, 190, 199
  wedding day preparations and confirmation,
    155, 156
vendor samples, 24–26, 154
volunteering, 15, 36, 94
volunteers as staffing support, 114

W
Web designers, 59
Web sites. *See also* Internet
  for bridal couple, 172, 180–81
  software for, 22
  for wedding planners, 61, 87, 88, 178–80, 183
  wedding trends, 182
wedding day organization
  checklist preparations, 149
  production schedule plans for, 141, 146–49
wedding planning businesses, overview
  benefits, 13
  industry growth of, 18
  as second job, 17–18
  top mistakes of, 17
Wedding Report, The, 10, 157
wedding statistics, 10–11, 157
women business owners, 177–78

About the Author

Jill S. Moran, CSEP, began her career in special event planning in 1990 by planning a client reception for 500 guests attending an international trade show. Drawing on her background in the arts, exhibit and display experience, and instinct for creativity and planning, she grew her event business to include nonprofits events, weddings, and social celebrations. She has helped clients with diverse events, from multiday destination weddings to tented seaside celebrations.

She has grown her award-winning event planning and management company, jsmoran special events, by providing creative advice and full-scale implementation and production services for special events ranging from corporate outings, and sales and marketing events to galas and exclusive parties. She has hosted events and weddings in cities across the country and internationally in locations ranging from museums and yachts to convention centers and wineries. Her events have been televised on Entertainment Tonight and E!. She has been showcased on Boston's Channel 7 WHDH-TV sharing design and party decorating ideas.

Jill has served on several international committees for ISES, the International Special Events Society, and has been president for the New England Chapter. She was one of the first designated Certified Special Event Professionals in the New England area and is passionate about professionalism in the industry. She was a 2003 winner of the prestigious ESPRIT award for excellence in event production and design and in 2005 was awarded an ESPRIT for Best Industry Contribution for her first book, *How to Start a Home-Based Event Planning Business*. She has lectured at Eventworld, The Special Event and ISES Regional Education Conferences and has participated on panel discussions for industry conferences throughout the United States and in Canada.

Her varied background includes a degree in Music Education, MBA coursework, and continued involvement in the arts and education on a community level. She lives in Massachusetts with her family and continues to enjoy creating the life of the party!